material obsession

KATHY DOUGHTY and SARAH FIELKE

PHOTOGRAPHY BY

JOHN DOUGHTY

FOREWORD BY KAFFE FASSETT

MURDOCH BOOKS

FOREWORD

Being in the business of teaching, lecturing and judging quilt shows around the world, I get to see a great variation in standards. I have experienced much less-than-inspiring work that takes up wall space in shops and exhibitions.

It was, therefore, a very special moment for me when I first encountered the small shop in Sydney that is Material Obsession. I was immediately taken with the imagination and taste level of the quilts on display. Having a workshop and lecture to give for them, I was able to witness Kathy and Sarah's shop in action and see how they shared their knowledge and talent with each of their customers, who appeared to be more like an extended family. Over the days I was there, we travelled into wilder parts of the area to get a real sense of the landscape that seems to feed their creative output. Climbing over great dinosaur bones of rocks on the beach, and driving through richly coloured fields and trees to arrive at a museum of a shop filled with antique quilts, buttons and embellishments gave me a taste of their quality of life. All this is important to us creative people who try to share our insights with others, because it gives us that base of happiness that spills over to those around us.

Quilting is a huge subject. It exercises our making skills, but much more importantly it can be a large canvas for expressing the emotions of our lives. In order for many of us to do this on a level that communicates with others, we need a great deal of encouragement and confidence building.

Sarah and Kathy are two quilt artists who not only own their shop and challenge their customers to deepen their knowledge of the craft, but who also both take time to break new ground in their quest for inspiration. This renews their creative juices and allows them to pass on what they discover.

There is another big reason why I am so taken with the activities around this shop. They have a great respect for traditional quilts. Not only a respect, but the talent to pour new life into these great old geometric layouts. This is a subject close to my heart, as I am constantly amazed by how much juice there is to be gleaned from these classic formulas. The world of textile prints comes to life in a special way when fed into these elegant structures. We are all helping to keep a very important tradition alive and available to many people around the world who crave the satisfaction of using their hands and skills to make things of beauty and harmony.

Kaffe Fassett

contents

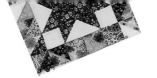

Introduction

Welcome to quilting the Material Obsession way. You may have made many quilts before, or none; but we'd like to think this book might inspire you to make some. And to have a lot of fun while you're at it!

Material Obsession came to be as a reflection of our times. Our quilts reflect a lifestyle that is moving quickly, and changing every day. Quilts were once a part of a slower-moving era, one of frugal use of leftovers and recycled fabrics, and time spent on necessary items for warmth and comfort. They were either small pieces of carefully chosen and fussy-cut geometric shapes, hand sewn and quilted over years, or large pieces thrown together, tied and much patched to create quick utilitarian items.

Quilters today are free to indulge in a huge range of colour, shape and texture, in large pieces and small. They recycle only where a design feature makes such a choice important. And they quilt for love, for enjoyment and for creativity rather than for necessity.

The questions we are most asked about our quilts always involve colour. How do we pick the fabrics we pick, how do we decide? Many people believe they aren't 'good with colour', or aren't 'creative'. We think everyone is good with colour, they just don't realise it. Being 'good with colour' is all about finding the things that inspire you in the world around you. The colours in a favourite flower, an animal's fur, a sunset — all the 'right' colour choices have already been made for you, you just need to know where to look.

Colour is like a magic wand. It speaks to us and screams YES or NO. There is a technical side to colour that can be taught, and which involves contrasting colours, complementary colours, shades, tones and everything in between. We believe the best way of using colour is by instinct. You know what looks good to you; make your personal choices from inside and trust how you feel about a colour combination.

Inspiration can spring from many places — a photo, a painting, a person, history, a picture in a magazine, or from existing quilts. If the inspiration sparks a memory for you, or links to an interest, you can make a start. Ask yourself some questions about why you are making the quilt in the first place, and you may find some answers.

The 'One' inspiration

What is it about quilts that invites you to make one? We always try to find that One reason, and it's a great way to spark off your quilting career. Do you like squares? Triangles? Scrappy quilts, or red and white? Do you want comfort, or history, or home decoration? Handwork or machine piecing? Who is the quilt for? What do you want it to reflect? All these things will help you decide the One place for you to start your quilt.

Starting with One fabric that makes you sing is one of our favourite ways to choose colours for a quilt. Find One fabric you love, perhaps a large floral with a combination of colours, and start there. We call this fabric the inspiration fabric.

Look at all the different colours in the fabric — and don't forget that there might be several shades of the one colour. All the colours the fabric has in it will enable you to choose your colour palette. Add some spots, or stripes, or different scale prints to co-ordinate and complement your initial fabric selection. Try not to worry that something is 'too spotty' or 'too busy'. Following traditional rules — such as having to use a plain fabric, or never putting blue and green together — will only put limits on your fun. A spot can act as a background or a neutral if used in the right way. If the fabrics look good to you, if you like them, then you have the beginnings of success.

In the same vein, don't be hung up on finding the exact same pink, the precise type of green. Nothing in nature uses the exact shade of a colour everywhere to make it beautiful. Nature combines many different shades of colours to make a lovely whole, and you can do the same in your quilts.

Graphics are an important part of our decision making. Antique quilts are usually made from fabrics employing small graphics, due to the fashion of the times. Nowadays, we have so many scales of pattern available to us it's almost dizzying. Varying the scale of the graphics in your quilt can play a huge part in the success of a design. Don't be afraid to cut large graphics up into small pieces to create different effects. Play with the idea that a large pattern can become many different small patterns if used in a different manner.

Having said all that, the one thing you can't ignore is contrast. Many a quilt has begun life with piles of yummy fabrics, been lovingly pieced, excitedly finished, stepped back from and ... where did all the blocks go? You must have light and dark to make your design work. If you are confused as to how to go about this, first make a line drawing of one of your blocks on a piece of paper. Look at the lines for a while, then shade the pieces which will make the block into a pattern. See the difference? If you do not make these pieces stand out, and they instead are of the same tonal value as the rest of the block, you won't have a pattern.

Seeing contrast in your fabrics is easy. Fabrics react to those that they are next to at any given moment. Pile your fabrics on a table and squint at them. The darker fabrics will pop out and the lighter ones will recede. If there's no popping or receding, you need more contrast. Another way to do this is to take several digital images of your fabrics piled in different combinations. Studying the photos will help you see what is missing.

Once you have a starting point, the rest is easier. Let's say your One starting point is a quilt for your mother. It's for her couch. She likes brown and aqua. You have found a large brown floral you like, which also has pink in it. So, you need big blocks to showcase the floral, aqua for your mum and pink for highlights. Get to it!

Antique quilts are a great source of ideas. However, they are often intricately pieced blocks, and your initial reaction might be to put them in the too-hard basket. Start thinking about how to make the design work for you. The easiest way to do this is to enlarge the block and make it easier to play with. This is something we do all the time, and it's a great way to make use of the wide range of large and colourful graphics that are available to quilters today.

All the quilts in this book were designed by us, and they all had a starting point. That point differs in each quilt, and we have attempted to explain to you what those points are to help you with your own decision making. Often our inspiration comes from fabrics rather than other sources — hey, we're surrounded by a shop full of amazing colour day in and day out, we can't be expected not to be tempted!

The most important thing we want you to remember about quilting as you read this book is that quilting doesn't have to be about boundaries. Some people have a rigid perception about quilting, believing that everything must be hand pieced, or hand quilted, or hand appliquéd, or done a certain way or to a certain size, or use certain colours or tones, or else it isn't a 'good' quilt. We encourage you not to think that way, and to be guided by your preferences and tastes. The best and most important decision you can make about your quilt is that it's yours, you did a great job, you love it and you're proud of it. Show the world! And have a great time while you're at it.

Kathy and Sarah

projects

Avalon

Kathy Doughty

EASY

THE IDEA

To start with, pick one fabric you love. Add other favourite fabrics that co-ordinate, and vary the scale — use spots, stripes, florals, geometrics … everything in one big block, shown off like a department store window.

An alternative colourway is shown on page 18.

Finished quilt size

King single, 165 x 220 cm (66 x 87 inches)
Finished block size: 18½ inches square including seam allowance

Materials and tools

Twelve 50 cm (20 inch) square fat quarters
1.5 m (60 inches) white fabric for sashing
4.4 m (176 inches) backing fabric
50 cm (20 inches) binding fabric
180 x 240 cm (72 x 96 inch) piece cotton wadding
Rotary cutter, ruler and mat
Neutral-coloured cotton thread for piecing
3–4 balls of perle cotton No 8, if hand quilting

NOTE: *It is recommended that all fabrics be 100 percent cotton, and be ironed. Requirements are based on fabric 112 cm (44 inches) wide. Unless otherwise stated, all seam allowances are ¼ inch throughout. Colour test any dark fabrics that you are using (see page 177), and wash them before cutting if they run. Please read all instructions before starting.*

Cutting

All fabrics are strip cut across the width of the fabric, from selvedge to fold (cut off all selvedges first).

FOR THE SQUARES, trim all of the fat quarters to 18½ inches square.

FROM THE SASHING FABRIC, cut fifteen strips 3½ inches wide.
   Cross cut four of these strips to yield eight pieces 3½ x 18½ inches.
Cut three of the remaining strips in half and join five of these half-pieces to five whole pieces. Trim to make five strips 3½ x 60½ inches for the cross-sashing strips and the top and bottom borders.
Cut one remaining strip in half. Join each half-piece end to end to one of the remaining strips for the side borders.

FROM THE BINDING FABRIC, cut eight strips 2½ inches wide and join them end to end on the diagonal (see page 196).

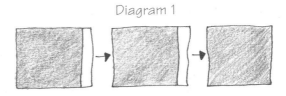

Diagram 1

Diagram 3

Diagram 2

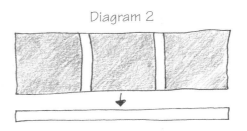

Sewing

Select your layout by arranging the squares on a flat surface or a design wall if possible. Check for colour and design balance. To do this, look through the lens of a camera, or even better, take a digital image.

Sew one 18½ inch long sashing strip to the right-hand side of the left and centre squares of each row (see Diagram 1). Sew all three sets together to form the top row, then do the same to form the second row, and so on.

To the bottom of each row, carefully pin one of the 60½ inch long cross-sashing strips (see Diagram 2). Then pin the last of these strips to the top of the top row, to form the top border. Carefully sew the strips to the rows, then sew all the rows together.

Borders

Measure through the length of the quilt to determine the exact outer border lengths (they should be 87½ inches). Trim the borders to fit. Find the middle of each of the borders and the middle of the body of the quilt, pin these points and then pin the ends. Pin throughout the length of each border in order to allow for any variations. Gently ease the edges as necessary to make them fit together. When the borders fit perfectly, sew them on (see Diagram 3). This method will ensure a flat border free of waves.

The quilt top is now complete. Press the entire quilt top carefully.

Backing, quilting and binding

When the top is complete, measure your backing fabric and cut to fit, allowing a little extra, and piecing it if necessary to get the right size.

Refer to pages 192–197 for instructions on finishing. This quilt was machine quilted in an edge-to-edge pattern.

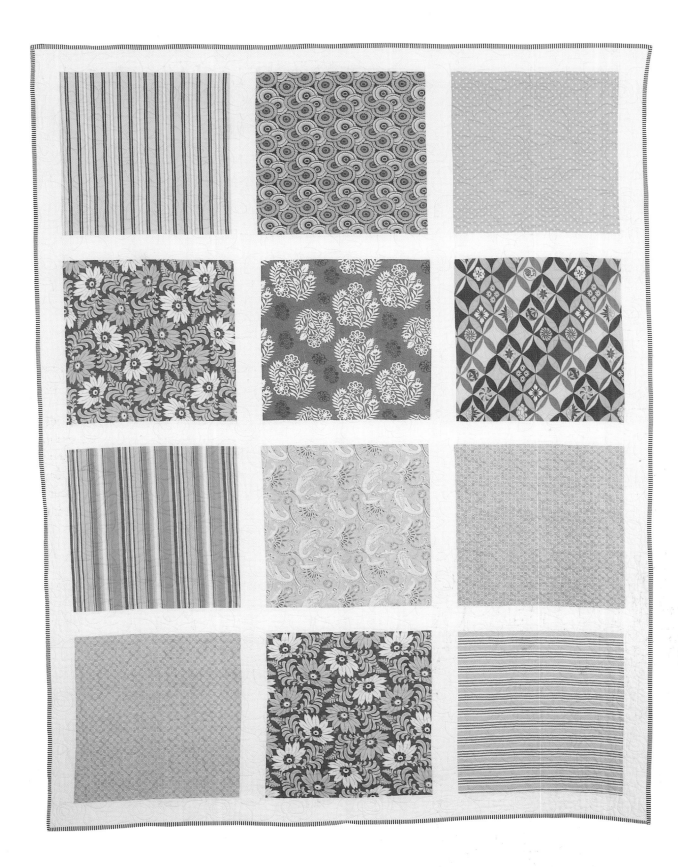

Gypsy Squares

Sarah Fielke   EASY

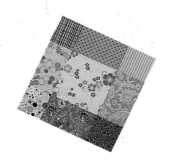

THE IDEA

One block and one of each of everything special you love in your stash and can't bear to cut up — all this equals one gorgeous quilt, one that's on my bed and is still my favourite one of all time. Instructions are given for three sizes.

The key to this quilt is in the size of the graphics. Make sure you have some large and some medium scale florals, some stripes and an assortment of small-scale prints, and everything will come up roses.

Finished quilt size

King, 280 cm (112 inches) square
Queen, 220 cm (96 inches) square
Throw, 160 cm (64 inches) square
Finished block size: 8½ inches square including seam allowance

Materials and tools

	King	Queen	Throw
25 cm (10 inch) strips	40	29	13
Backing fabric	9 m (10 yards)	7.2 m (8 yards)	3.6 m (4 yards)
Binding fabric	85 cm (35 inches)	70 cm (28 inches)	50 cm (20 inches)
Cotton wadding	3 m (3⅓ yds) square	2.4 m (2⅔ yds) square	1.8 m (2 yds) square

Rotary cutter, ruler and mat
Neutral-coloured cotton thread for piecing
Sewing machine
General sewing supplies
Perle cotton No 8 for quilting (the number of balls you need will depend on the size of the quilt and the extent of the quilting)

NOTE: *It is recommended that all fabrics be 100 percent cotton, and be ironed. Requirements are based on fabric 112 cm (44 inches) wide. Unless otherwise stated, all seam allowances are ¼ inch throughout. Colour test any dark fabrics that you are using (see page 177), and wash them before cutting if they run. Please read all instructions before starting.*

Cutting

All fabrics are strip cut across the width of the fabric, from selvedge to fold (cut off all selvedges first).

FOR THE SQUARES, cut all the fabrics into 8½ inch strips and cross cut these into squares. You will need 196 squares for king size, 144 squares for queen size and 64 squares for a throw.

FROM THE BINDING FABRIC, cut 2½ inch strips.

Sewing

Select your layout by putting the squares on a flat surface. Check for colour and design balance. To do this, look through the lens of a camera, or even better, take a digital image.

To assemble, pin each block to the next across the rows. Using a ¼ inch seam, piece all the rows and then join them together, being careful to match the seams at the corners. You may want to number the rows to keep track of placement.

For king size, each row should have 14 blocks.

For queen size, each row should have 12 blocks.

For throw size, each row should have 8 blocks.

Press the seams in alternate directions: on the first row press them to the right, on the second row to the left, and so on. This will help you to make a clean join at the corners and to reduce bulk in the seams.

Press the entire quilt top carefully.

Backing, quilting and binding

When the top is complete, measure your backing fabric and cut to fit, allowing a little extra, and piecing it if necessary to get the right size.

See pages 192–197 for instructions on finishing.

This quilt was quilted in perle cotton No 8, with the fabric pattern directing the quilting design in each block. If there are flowers, you can quilt around them. If there are stripes, quilt along the stripes. Meander the quilting line around each block, and be creative!

This is a quick and simple quilt to piece, so you can afford to spend the time on quilting to make it really special.

Candy Shop

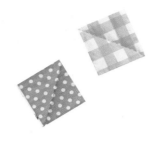

Sarah Fielke

EASY

THE IDEA

Candy Shop was our first pattern, and is one of our most successful. The idea for it came from the sweet, fresh fabric. I had just come out of a long stay in hospital and the fabrics were breezing through my bad mood, reminding me of cherries and bunches of flowers, and even though I hadn't sewn for nearly four months I just had to sit down and start. I made this top in an afternoon.

Many of our beginners start with this quilt. They all love the idea of quilting the motifs into the plain squares. It looks good made in every colour of the rainbow, which is about how many we've seen it in. This quilt is so popular, we've developed a king single version, too, called Corner Shop (see page 30).

Finished quilt size
Throw, 130 cm (52 inches) square

Materials and tools

30 cm (12 inches) white quilter's muslin
30 cm (12 inches) of ten different fabrics for the triangles and outer border
20 cm (8 inches) blue patterned fabric for the inner border
3 m (120 inches) backing fabric
40 cm (16 inches) binding fabric
150 cm (60 inch) square piece cotton wadding
Rotary cutter, ruler and mat
Neutral-coloured cotton thread for piecing
2B pencil and sharpener
Perle cotton No 8 in pink, blue, yellow and mint green
Crewel embroidery needle No 9

NOTE: *It is recommended that all fabrics be 100 percent cotton, and be ironed. Requirements are based on fabric 112 cm (44 inches) wide. Unless otherwise stated, all seam allowances are ¼ inch throughout. Colour test any dark fabrics that you are using (see page 177), and wash them before cutting if they run. Please read all instructions before starting.*

Cutting

All fabrics are strip cut across the width of the fabric, from selvedge to fold.

FROM THE QUILTER'S MUSLIN, cut sixteen 5½ inch squares.

FROM THE TEN ASSORTED PATTERNED FABRICS, CUT:

A total of thirty-two 4½ inch squares for Broken Dishes block triangles. Cut these squares in half along one diagonal to form sixty-four half-square triangles.

A total of sixty-four 5½ inch squares for the outer border.

FROM THE INNER BORDER FABRIC, cut four 1½ inch strips.

FROM SCRAPS, cut four 1½ inch squares for corners of inner border.

FROM THE BINDING FABRIC, cut 2½ inch strips.

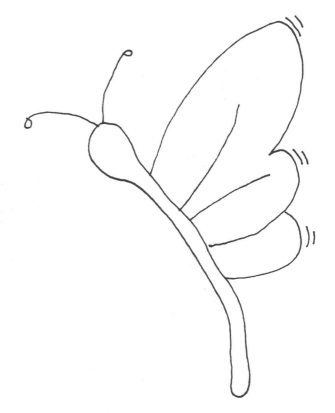

Preparation

Using a light box or a sunny window, lightly trace the quilting patterns (see the diagrams on these pages and page 28) onto each muslin square using a sharp 2B pencil, remembering that the squares are set on point. To prevent the pencil marks from settling into the fibres of the fabric and becoming difficult to remove, do not use a back-and-forth sketching motion with your pencil; instead, draw a single line. Refer to the photo on page 29 for the placement of the quilted blocks, or invent your own arrangement.

Sewing

Use a ¼ inch seam throughout.

For the centre panel, mixing the fabrics well, stitch a triangle to each side of the muslin square along the bias edge by finding the centre of the long edge of the triangle, and the centre of the edge of the square. Pin these points together. The ends of the triangle will extend beyond the edge of the square to allow for seam allowance (see Diagram 1, page 28). Press the seams away from the muslin and trim the 'ears' off the triangles. Repeat in this manner until you have sixteen Broken Dishes blocks. See Diagram 2, page 28).

Join the blocks together in pairs, then join two pairs together to form a four-patch, taking care to match the seams. Make four units of four, then join these together to form the sixteen-block centre panel.

For the inner border, measure each side of the centre panel and trim if the edges are not straight. Cut the 1½ inch strips to fit the sides. Find the centre of the strip and the centre of the panel, match these points and pin. Next pin the ends, then pin in between, gently easing as needed to make the pieces fit together. Sew. Repeat for the other side of the inner border.

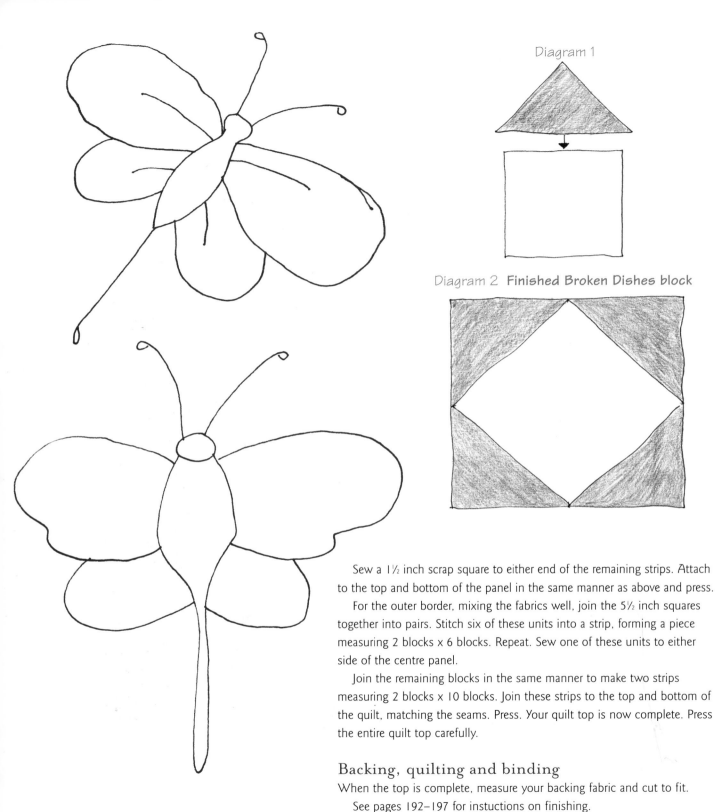

Diagram 1

Diagram 2 **Finished Broken Dishes block**

Sew a 1½ inch scrap square to either end of the remaining strips. Attach to the top and bottom of the panel in the same manner as above and press.

For the outer border, mixing the fabrics well, join the 5½ inch squares together into pairs. Stitch six of these units into a strip, forming a piece measuring 2 blocks x 6 blocks. Repeat. Sew one of these units to either side of the centre panel.

Join the remaining blocks in the same manner to make two strips measuring 2 blocks x 10 blocks. Join these strips to the top and bottom of the quilt, matching the seams. Press. Your quilt top is now complete. Press the entire quilt top carefully.

Backing, quilting and binding

When the top is complete, measure your backing fabric and cut to fit.

See pages 192–197 for instructions on finishing.

This quilt was hand quilted with the motifs supplied in the plain squares, and diagonal lines running through the other squares.

Corner Shop

Kathy Doughty   EASY

THE IDEA

Candy Shop, our first pattern, was
such a hit we decided to make a
bigger version, this time in 1930s
prints in red, yellow and blue.
Everyone has a stash of 1930s
or fun, bright fabrics just waiting
for a perfect pattern like this to
bring them to life.

Finished quilt size
King single, 153 x 216 cm (60 x 85 inches)

Materials and tools
60 cm (24 inches) white quilter's muslin
30 cm (12 inches) each of 10 different fabrics for triangles and outer border
30 cm (12 inches) red stripe fabric for inner border
4.5 m (5 yards) backing fabric
50 cm (20 inches) binding fabric
170 x 240 cm (68 x 95 inch) piece of cotton wadding
Rotary cutter, mat and ruler
Neutral-coloured cotton thread for piecing
Perle cotton No 8 in pink, blue, yellow and mint green
Crewel embroidery needle No 9

NOTE: *It is recommended that all fabrics be 100 percent cotton,
and be ironed. Requirements are based on fabric 112 cm
(44 inches) wide. Unless otherwise stated, all seam allowances
are ¼ inch throughout. Colour test any dark fabrics that you are
using (see page 177), and wash them before cutting if they run.
Please read all instructions before starting.*

Cutting
All fabrics are strip cut across the width of the fabric, from selvedge to fold
(cut off all selvedges first).

FROM THE QUILTER'S MUSLIN, cut thirty 5½ inch squares.

FROM THE TEN ASSORTED PATTERNED FABRICS, CUT:
A total of sixty 4½ inch squares for the block triangles. Cut these squares
   in half along one diagonal to form 120 half-square triangles.
A total of 132 5½ inch squares for the outer border.

FROM THE INNER BORDER FABRIC, cut two 3 x 42½ inch strips
   and two 2 x 40½ inch strips.

FROM SCRAPS, cut four 1½ inch squares for corners of inner border.

FROM THE BINDING FABRIC, cut seven 2½ inch strips.

Preparation

Using a light box or a sunny window, lightly trace the quilting patterns (see these pages and page 35) onto each muslin square using a sharp 2B pencil, remembering that the squares are set on point. To prevent the pencil marks from settling into the fibres of the fabric and becoming difficult to remove, do not use a back-and-forth sketching motion with your pencil; instead, draw a single line. Refer to the photo on page 37 for the placement of the quilted blocks, or invent your own arrangement.

Sewing

Use a ¼ inch seam allowance throughout.

For the centre panel, mixing the fabrics well, stitch a triangle to each side of a muslin square along the bias edge (see Diagram 1, page 36). Press the seams away from the muslin and trim the 'ears' off the triangles. Repeat until you have 30 Broken Dishes blocks (see Diagram 2, page 36).

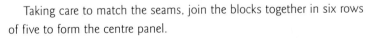

Taking care to match the seams, join the blocks together in six rows of five to form the centre panel.

For the inner border, measure each side of the centre panel and trim if the edges are not straight. Confirm that your inner border strips fit the sides. Find the centre of the strip and the centre of the edge of the panel, match these points and pin. Pin the ends, then pin in between, easing as necessary to make the pieces fit together. Sew. Repeat for the other side.

For the outer border, sew two sets of nine pairs of squares. Sew these sets to both sides of the centre panel. Make two sets of 12 rows of four squares for the top and bottom. Assemble as per the photograph and attach to the top and bottom, matching seam points where necessary.

The quilt top is now finished. Press the entire quilt top carefully.

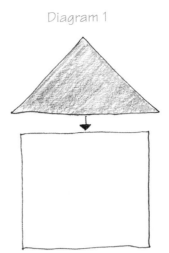

Diagram 1

Diagram 2 **Finished Broken Dishes block**

Backing, quilting and binding

When the top is complete, measure your backing fabric and cut to fit, allowing a little extra, and piecing it if necessary to get the right size.

See pages 192–197 for instrucitons on finishing.

This quilt was hand quilted using perle cotton No 8 in red, blue and yellow using the designs provided, or you can use your own designs for the plain squares. The coloured squares were quilted using masking tape to make diagonal lines through the squares in both directions.

Cowboy Baby

Kathy Doughty   EASY

THE IDEA

Cowboys and patchwork go hand in hand for baby boys. The pinwheels keep it active, and although it looks a bit tricky, the piecing is simple.

As this is a quilt for a baby, fabric choices are easy. The 1930s ranges are always fantastic, especially when used with a red and white spot. Children's prints with matching co-ordinates for the pinwheels will make any new mother happy.

Finished quilt size

Cot quilt, 100 x 120 cm (40 x 48 inches)
Finished block size: 8½ inches including seam allowance

Materials and tools

50 cm (20 inches) large cowboy print for outer border
20 cm (10 inches) stripe fabric for inner border
70 cm (30 inches) smaller all-over cowboy print for rectangles
25 cm (10 inches) light red check pattern for pinwheels
25 cm (10 inches) dark red print for pinwheels
25 cm (10 inches) light brown stripe fabric for pinwheels
25 cm (10 inches) dark brown print for pinwheels
20 cm (10 inches) red spot fabric for squares
20 cm (10 inches) light brown check fabric for squares
40 cm (20 inches) brown fabric for binding
1.2 x 1.3 m (48 x 52 inch) piece cotton wadding
1.3 m (52 inches) backing fabric
Half-square ruler (optional; if not using it, see note below under 'Cutting')
General sewing supplies
1 ball white perle cotton No 8 for quilting

NOTE: *It is recommended that all fabrics be 100 percent cotton, and be ironed. Requirements are based on fabric 112 cm (44 inches) wide. Unless otherwise stated, all seam allowances are ¼ inch throughout. Colour test any dark fabrics that you are using (see page 177); if they run, wash them before cutting. Please read all instructions before starting.*

Cutting

NOTE: *When cutting with the ruler, cut all strips, place them front sides together and cross cut using the ruler into half-square triangles. The instructions are written for using the ruler, but if you are not, all of the half-square triangles should be cut 2⅞ inches rather than 2 ½ inches. If you are not using the ruler,*

Diagram 1

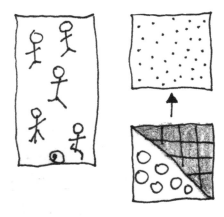

Diagram 2

Diagram 3

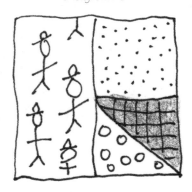

you should still place the strips face to face and cross cut 2⅞ inch squares, then cut along the diagonal to form the half-square triangles. Sew along the diagonal and press open in both cases.

FROM THE LARGE COWBOY FABRIC FOR THE BORDER, cut two 3½ x 40 inch strips and two 3½ x 48 inch strips.

FROM THE STRIPE FABRIC FOR THE INNER BORDER, cut two 1½ x 40 inch strips and two 1½ x 48 inch strips.

FROM THE COWBOY PRINT FOR THE RECTANGLES, cut ten 2½ inch strips, then cross cut these into eighty 2½ x 4½ inch rectangles.

FROM EACH OF THE FABRICS FOR THE PINWHEELS:

If you are not using the ruler, cut three 2⅞ inch strips, then match the light and dark strips in pairs. Cross cut into 20 squares, then cut the squares in half along one diagonal.

If you are using the ruler, cut three 2½ inch strips of all four fabrics. Match the light and dark fabrics with right sides facing. Using a 45-degree ruler, cut along the diagonal to form right-angle triangles. These pairs will be sewn with ¼ inch seams along the diagonal, starting with the blunt end.

FROM THE LIGHT BROWN CHECK FABRIC, cut three 2½ inch strips, then cross cut these to yield forty 2½ inch squares.

FROM THE LIGHT RED SPOT FABRIC, cut three 2½ inch strips, then cross cut these to yield forty 2½ inch squares.

FROM THE BINDING FABRIC, cut five 2½ inch strips.

Sewing

The 8-inch block comprises four sets, each set consisting of one 2½ x 4½ inch rectangle, one pinwheel and one 2½ inch square. See Diagram 4.

Make the pinwheel units first by sewing one dark and one light half-square triangle together. Sew the dark side of this unit to the square, with the light triangle of the pinwheel pointing to the top left-hand corner (see Diagram 1). Sew the rectangle to this set on the light side of the pinwheel (see Diagram 2).

This completes the unit (see Diagram 3).

Make four units and lay them out so that the dark points of the pinwheel point to the centre (see Diagram 4). Sew the two units on the right side, then the two units on the left side, and then join the halves, being careful to pin and match all points. This completes the block.

Make 10 red pinwheel blocks and 10 brown.

Assembly

Lay out the blocks, four across and five down, alternating the brown and red pinwheels as shown in the photograph on page 43. Pin, matching the seams, and sew together to form the horizontal rows.

Diagram 4 **Finished block**

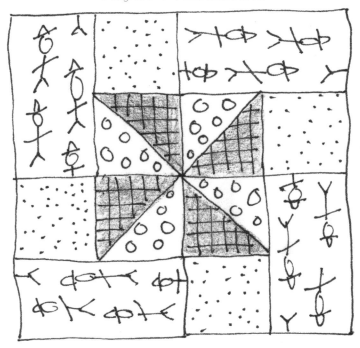

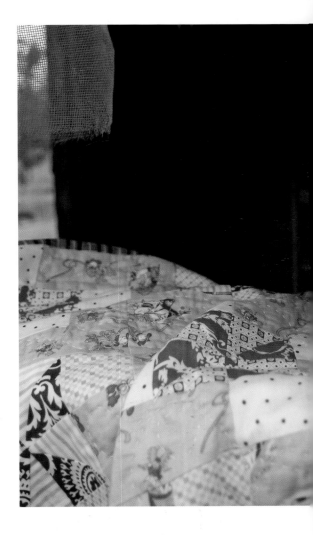

Starting with the top row, pin the rows together, matching the seams. Sew the rows together to form the body of the quilt.

Borders

Start with the side inner border pieces (the stripe fabric) and sew each along its length to the side outer border strip (the cowboy print).

Find the centre of the inner border strip and finger-press a crease. Find the centre of the body of the quilt and finger-press a crease. Match these points and pin together. Pin the ends flush to meet, and then continue pinning every few inches into the middle, gently easing the edges as necessary to make them fit together. When you have made the borders fit perfectly, sew them on. This method will ensure that your quilt is square and that the borders are flat and free of waves.

Repeat for the top and bottom borders.

Press the entire quilt top carefully.

Backing, quilting and binding

When the top is complete, measure your backing fabric and cut to fit, allowing a little extra. See pages 192–197 for instructions on finishing.

This quilt was quilted using perle cotton, following lines drawn with chalk to to look like a lasso running through all the rectangles.

Goodnight Sweet Prints

Sarah Fielke 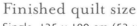 EASY

THE IDEA

This is an easy, quick one-patch quilt for little girls. It's fun to make and great for beginners.

You could easily make this quilt for a little boy instead by using reds, blues and greens with a car or truck panel replacing the flowers; or have a go with appliqué.

Finished quilt size

Single, 135 x 190 cm (53 x 75 inches)

Materials and tools

6 Prints Charming feature panels, approximately 50 cm (20 inches) square prior to trimming, or fat quarters with an interesting pattern
25 cm (10 inches) each of 11 different pink, purple and cream fabrics for the four-patch blocks
3.1 m (3½ yards) backing fabric
50 cm (20 inches) purple stripe fabric for binding
155 x 210 cm (61 x 83 inch) piece cotton wadding
Rotary cutter, ruler and mat
Neutral-coloured cotton thread for piecing
2B pencil and sharpener
Perle cotton No 8 in pink, green, purple and white for quilting

NOTE: *It is recommended that all fabrics be 100 percent cotton, and be ironed. Requirements are based on fabric 112 cm (44 inches) wide. Unless otherwise stated, all seam allowances are ¼ inch throughout. Colour test any dark fabrics that you are using (see page 177); if they run, wash them before cutting.*
Please read all instructions before starting.

Cutting

All strips are cut across the width of the fabric (from selvedge to fold).
TRIM EACH OF THE SIX FEATURE PANELS to 16½ inches square, ensuring that the design is in the centre.
FROM EACH OF THE FOUR-PATCH FABRICS, cut two 4½ inch strips. Cross cut these strips into eighteen squares. You should have 184 squares in total.
FROM THE BINDING FABRIC, cut seven 2½ inch strips.

Sewing

NOTE: *To save time, the pairs of squares and the four-patch units can all be chain-pieced (see page 190).*

Sew the squares into pairs, mixing the colours well.

Matching the centre seams, sew the pairs into four-patch blocks.

Sew the four-patches into rows, again taking care to mix the colours well so the same two do not appear together. Make four rows containing seven four-patch blocks in each row. (Each row will be 14 squares long by two squares high.) See Diagram 1.

Using the remaining four-patches, make nine units each containing two four-patches, making an eight-square unit. (Each unit will be two squares across by four squares down).

Stitch the long side of an eight-square unit to both sides of a feature panel. Stitch a feature panel to the right-hand side of the second unit, and another eight-square unit to the other side of the second feature panel. You should have a strip that reads thus: unit, panel, unit, panel, unit.

Repeat with the other feature panels until you have three such strips.

Join a 14-square strip to a panel strip and continue thus, alternating, until you have a finished quilt top. Take care to match the corners where the four-patch blocks meet. Press the entire quilt top carefully.

Backing, quilting and binding

When the top is complete, measure your backing fabric and cut to fit, allowing a little extra, and piecing it if necessary to get the right size.

See pages 192–197 for instructions on finishing.

The panels in this quilt were outline quilted by hand using pink, green and purple perle cotton No 8. The squares were cross hatched using masking tape to indicate the quilting lines, and hand quilted in white perle cotton No 8.

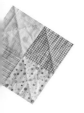

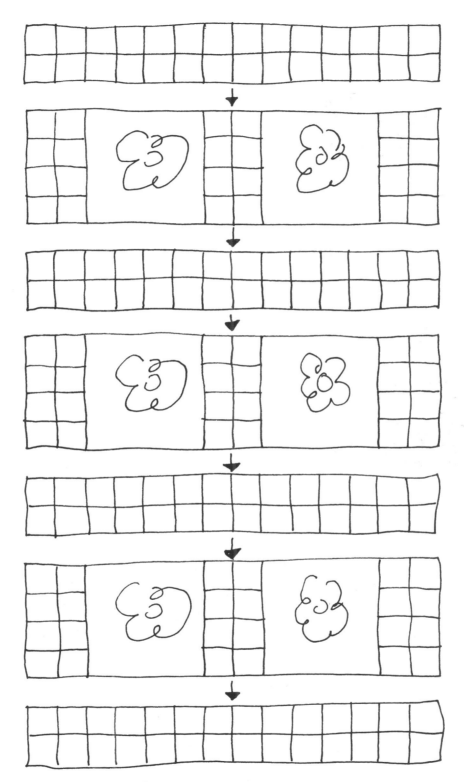

Diagram 1 **Quilt construction**

Retro Starburst

Kathy Doughty   EASY

THE IDEA

This quilt was designed to reflect the feeling of the large starburst blocks from Prints Charming. However, the blocks can be anything you choose. Look for big graphics, big flowers or bold spots. The Courthouse Steps blocks need contrast, so look for fabrics that vary in value. Include light, dark and everything in between, as well as a variety of colours.

The placement of the light and dark fabrics varies within and between the blocks, giving a touch of randomness to the quilt's structure.

The blocks are bold in construction, so this is a good choice for a boy, or a not-so-girly girl. Having said that, it would probably also look great with huge flowers and pink to red strips.

Finished quilt size

King single, 150 x 225 cm (59 x 89 inches)
Finished block size: 18½ inches square including seam allowance

Materials and tools

4 Prints Charming feature panels, approximately 47 cm (18½ inches) square prior to trimming; or fat quarters with an interesting pattern
2.5 m (3 yards) assorted light fabrics
2.5 m (3 yards) assorted dark fabrics
90 cm (36 inches) border fabric
5 m (5½ yards) backing fabric
60 cm (24 inches) binding fabric
Rotary cutter, ruler and mat
Neutral-coloured cotton thread for piecing
1.7 x 2.5 m (1¾ x 2¾ yard) piece cotton wadding
1 ball brown perle cotton No 8 for quilting

NOTE: *It is recommended that all fabrics be 100 percent cotton, and be ironed. Requirements are based on fabric 112 cm (44 inches) wide. Unless otherwise stated, all seam allowances are ¼ inch throughout. Colour test any dark fabrics that you are using (see page 177); if they run, wash them before cutting.*

Please read all instructions before starting.

Cutting

All fabrics are strip cut across the width of the fabric, from selvedge to fold (cut off all selvedges first).

The following cutting instructions are labelled alphabetically, but cut the largest pieces first and use the remaining fabric to cut the smaller strips.

BLOCK A

Trim the four feature panels to 18½ inches square and set aside.

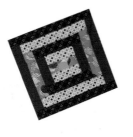

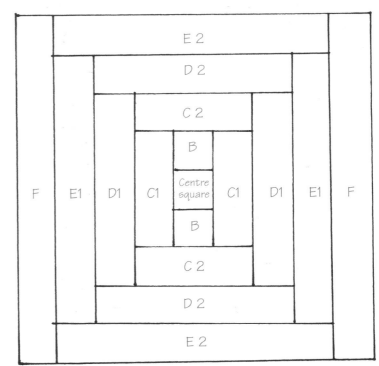

Diagram 1 **Block B piecing layout**

BLOCK B

Cut all the Block B fabrics (the assorted light and dark fabrics) into
2½ inch strips. Cut the longest pieces first and the smaller pieces from
the remainders, as follows. It is helpful to build one block at a time and
sew it together, then proceed to the next one.

FOR EACH BLOCK B (CUT 11 SETS IN THIS MANNER):
Cut one 2½ inch square for the centre (A).
Cut two 2½ inch contrast squares (B).
Cut two light (C1) and two dark (C2) strips 6½ inches long.
Cut two light (D1) and two dark (D2) strips 10½ inches long.
Cut two light (E1) and two dark (E2) strips 14½ inches long.
Cut two light or dark strips 18½ inches long (F).

BORDERS AND BINDING

FROM THE BORDER FABRIC, cut five strips 6½ inches wide. Sew
them end to end and cut in half widthways. Trim them to fit the five
rows once they are assembled. Each border should equal 90½ inches
in length.

FROM THE BINDING FABRIC, cut eight strips 3 inches long.

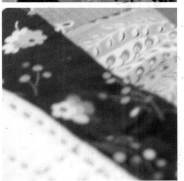

Sewing: Block B

See Diagram 1 for the piecing layout for Block B. Make 11 blocks.

Arrange your strips into eleven piles of contrasting strips and one centre square. Lay each block out with contrasting C1/C2, D1/D2, E1/E2 and two F strips. To make the quilt look more organised, plan your blocks to strictly work in light and dark directions from the centre. To keep the retro madness feel, work the colours by alternating the light and dark sides from the centre (that is, ending with a light F in some blocks and a dark F in others).

Start with a centre square.

Sew a B square to opposite sides of the centre square.

Sew a C1 strip to both sides of this set.

Sew a C2 strip to both ends of this set.

Sew a D1 strip to both sides of this set.

Sew a D2 to both ends of this set.

Do the same with the E1 and E2 strips and then finish with an F strip on each side.

The finished block should be square and measure 18½ inches all round.

Quilt construction

Construct the body of the quilt by sewing five rows of three blocks. Set out the feature panels in the centre or rows 2 and 4 and on the ends of row three (refer to the photograph on page 55).

Borders

For the borders, measure the width and the length through the centre of the quilt body. Trim the border pieces to 90½ inches after checking to make sure your sewing is accurate. Find the middle of the border strips and finger-press a crease. Find the middle of the body of the quilt and finger-press a crease. Match these points and pin. Pin the ends, then pin every few inches along the sides to allow for any variations. Gently ease the edges as necessary to make them fit together. When you have made the borders fit perfectly, sew them on. This method will ensure a flat border free of waves. Press flat, towards the borders.

Press the entire quilt top carefully.

Backing, quilting and binding

When the top is complete, measure your backing fabric and cut to fit, allowing a little extra, and piecing it if necessary to get the right size.

See pages 192–197 for instructions on finishing.

This quilt was hand quilted by setting out rectangles using masking tape and quilting around the inside and the outside of the tape with brown perle cotton.

Smuggling Letters

Kathy Doughty   INTERMEDIATE

THE IDEA

The block in this quilt jumped out of a Civil War Diaries book. The quilt is made using a bias rectangle ruler to simplify construction.

I love making up kits for this quilt using sweet floral fabrics. The blocks look so much like pretty little bows in rows. They can be all the same, or try using lots of small patterned pinks. The background fabric pictured has a lively floral print that keeps the pattern interesting.

Finished quilt size

King single, 145 x 225 cm (58 x 90 inches)
Finished block size: 15½ inches square including seam allowance

Materials and tools

40 cm (16 inches) for the centre squares and cornerstones
1.7 m (68 inches) light blue fabric
1.7 m (68 inches) red fabric
3.2 m (3½ yards) background fabric
5.6 m (6⅛ yards) backing fabric
50 cm (20 inches) binding fabric
170 x 240 cm (1¾ x 2⅔ yards) piece cotton wadding
Nifty Notions bias rectangle ruler and half-square ruler (optional)
Rotary cutter, ruler and mat
Neutral-coloured cotton thread for piecing
Perle cotton No 8 in cream, red and blue for quilting

NOTE: *It is recommended that all fabrics be 100 percent cotton, and be ironed. Requirements are based on fabric 112 cm (44 inches) wide. Unless otherwise stated, all seam allowances are ¼ inch throughout. Colour test any dark fabrics that you are using (see page 177); if they run, wash them before cutting.*
Please read all instructions before starting.

Cutting

NOTE: *Instructions are given for cutting with or without the bias rectangle ruler and the half-square ruler. Those for using the rulers are written first. If you are not using these rulers, disregard these instructions so as not to confuse yourself, and use the templates provided.*

All fabrics are strip cut across the width of the fabric, from selvedge to fold (cut off all selvedges first). Cut the largest pieces first.

MAIN BLOCKS (MAKE 8 BLUE AND 7 RED)

As these blocks require several different pieces, it is a good idea to put each different type of piece in a lock-seal plastic bag labelled A, B, C etc. This will save confusion and keep the pieces tidy. It is also helpful to make one block up and keep it as a reference as you make the rest of the blocks.

A. SQUARES Cut ten strips of the background fabric 3½ inches wide, then cross cut these into 120 squares, or eight per block.

B. HALF-SQUARE TRIANGLES *If you are using the half-square ruler*, cut ten strips 3½ inches wide of background fabric and five each of the red and blue. Match all background strips with a red or blue strip, right sides facing. Line up the blunt end of the ruler with the top of the strip. Line up the 3½ inch dotted line with the bottom of the strip and cut along the diagonal side of the ruler. Flip the ruler so the blunt end is on the bottom of the strip and cut again. Continue until you have 64 blue half-square triangle squares and 56 red.

If you are not using the half-square ruler, cut the above strips 3⅞ inches wide. Match them with right sides together and cross cut into squares, then in half along one diagonal. You will need 64 blue half-square triangles and 56 red.

C. COLOURED SQUARES Cut three strips 3½ inches wide in each of the red and blue fabrics. Cross cut into 28 red squares and 32 blue.

D. BIAS SQUARES *If you are using the bias square ruler*, cut four strips 3½ inches wide in the blue fabric, fold in half lengthwise with wrong sides facing, then use the narrow side of the bias square ruler to cut the right and left points at the same time. Cut 32 sets of blue. Repeat for 28 sets of the red fabric. These are the bias square points (D and DR).

Cut five strips 3½ inches wide in the background fabric, then use the wide side of the bias square ruler to cut 60 triangles. These are the bias square centres (DC).

If you are not using the bias square ruler, trace Templates D, DR and DC onto plastic or paper to use as a cutting guide.

E. BLOCK CENTRE SQUARE Cut two strips 3½ inches wide for the centre squares and cross cut into 15 squares.

F. CORNERSTONES Cut two strips 3½ inches wide in the centre square fabric for the sashing cornerstones. Cross cut these into squares.

NOTE: These can be in the same fabric as the centre square of the block, or use a splash of colour from your stash.

G. SASHING Cut eight strips 1¾ inches wide in the red fabric, then cross cut into strips 15½ inches long. Do the same in the blue. Cut 38 pairs.

H. BORDERS Cut five strips 3½ inches wide. Sew them end to end and then cut in half widthways. Once the quilt top is complete, trim the borders to the length of the quilt, which should measure 90 inches.

BINDING Cut eight strips 2½ inches wide for the binding.

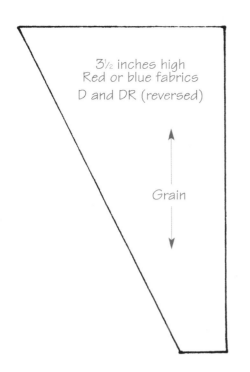

3½ inches high
Red or blue fabrics
D and DR (reversed)

↑
Grain
↓

Template for D and DR **Bias square sides**

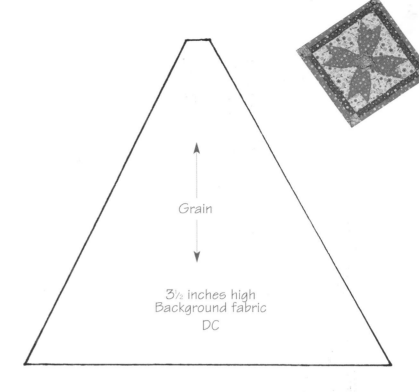

↑
Grain
↓

3½ inches high
Background fabric
DC

Template for DC **Bias square centre**

Diagram 1 **Block pattern**

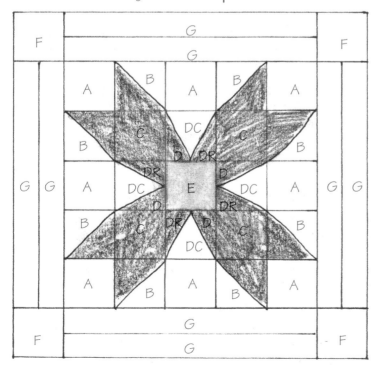

Sewing

Review the block pattern (Diagram 1, page 59) carefully.

Sew the half-square triangles together in sets along the diagonal line starting with the blunt corner. Press flat without stretching.

Sew the right side (D), then the left side (DR) of each of the bias triangles to the middle triangle (DC). Press flat without stretching.

Lay out the blocks as shown in the diagram, one at a time. Sew the blocks together in five rows of five as shown in the photograph opposite. Match all points and sew the blocks together by first assembling one block and using it as a reference to do the remaining fourteen blocks.

Sew the red and blue sashing strips together in 38 pairs. Lay out the blocks in horizontal rows and place the sashing strips between them, alternating the direction of the blue and red strips. The rows should start and end with sashing strips.

Lay out the rest of the sashing strips for the horizontal sashing rows, alternating with a cornerstone square. Each row should start and end with a cornerstone square and have three sashing strips.

Assemble the rows from top to bottom by lining up all the corner seams. Press the entire quilt top carefully.

Backing, quilting and binding

When the top is complete, measure your backing fabric and cut to fit, allowing a little extra, and piecing it if necessary to get the right size.

See pages 192–197 for instructions on finishing.

The pictured example was hand quilted using perle cotton No 8 in cream, red and blue ½ inch outside the seams.

Annie's Garden

Sarah Fielke

THE IDEA

Inspired by a friend's little girl, Annie, who loves pretty things and pink and purple things. I designed the quilt for her mother to make for her; mine is finished and hers has been in a bag for five years!

This is easy appliqué for beginners. There is a lot of work involved, but it is not difficult and the results are worth the effort. It's also a good way to use up scraps. If you don't have a large selection of scraps in the desired colours, buy 10–15 fat quarters and see how you go from there.

What ties this quilt together is the red; take it away and you miss it instantly, as it packs a punch. This is something to remember when you're choosing fabrics for your garden.

Finished quilt size

King single, 150 x 200 cm (59 x 79 inches)

Materials and tools

1 m (40 inches) white tone-on-tone fabric

75 cm (30 inches) red and white pin-dot fabric for inner border and binding

Six 25 cm (10 inch) pieces of fabric for backgrounds, in pink and purple. The fabrics can be striped, checked or plain, but ensure that they are not too boldly patterned or the appliqué will not show up against them

25 cm (10 inches) of a minimum of ten fabrics for pinwheels, four-patches and appliqué

Assortment of green fabrics for grass and stems, or 40 cm (16 inches) green fabric

2 m (80 inches) Vliesofix (see Hint below)

2B pencil and sharpener

DMC stranded embroidery cotton in colours to match appliqué fabrics, if blanket-stitching by hand; or machine embroidery cottons, if using machine blanket stitch

3.4 m (3¾ yards) backing fabric

170 x 220 cm (68 x 88 inches) piece cotton wadding

Perle cotton No 8 in pink for quilting

NOTE: *It is recommended that all fabrics be 100 percent cotton, and be ironed. Requirements are based on fabric 112 cm (44 inches) wide. Unless otherwise stated, all seam allowances are ¼ inch throughout. Colour test any dark fabrics that you are using (see page 177); if they run, wash them before cutting. Please read all instructions before starting.*

HINT: *Do not ever fold Vliesofix. Folding will cause the webbing to come away from the paper and render the Vliesofix useless. If you have never used Vliesofix before, please read the instructions carefully before beginning.*

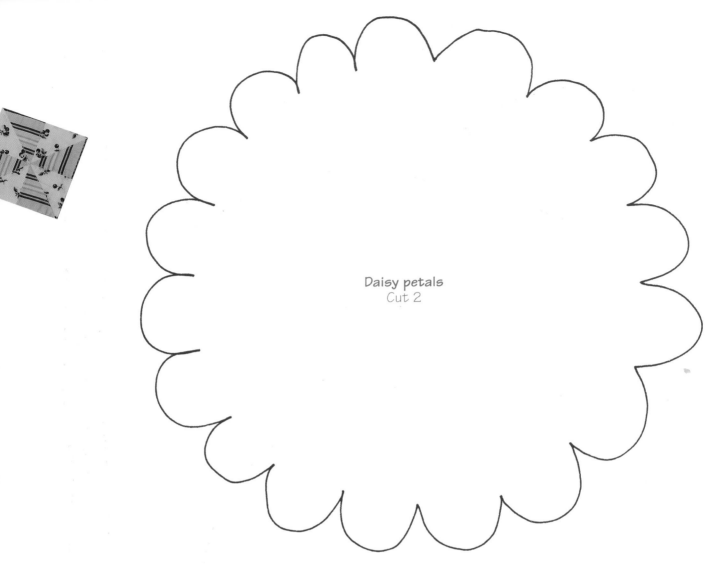

Daisy petals
Cut 2

Cutting

All fabrics are strip cut across the width of the fabric, from selvedge to fold (cut off all selvedges first).

FROM THE TONE-ON-TONE FABRIC, CUT:

Two strips 8½ inches wide. Cross cut these strips to yield ten squares for the outer border.

Five strips 4½ inches wide. Cross cut these strips to yield forty-four squares for the four-patches.

FROM THE RED AND WHITE PIN DOT FABRIC, CUT:

Four 2½ inch strips for the inner border.

Eight 2½ inch strips for the binding.

THE ASSORTED 25 CM STRIPS OF FABRIC are meant to be used for three purposes — pinwheel pieces, four-patches and appliqué flowers — so mix everything up to ensure that you get all three types of

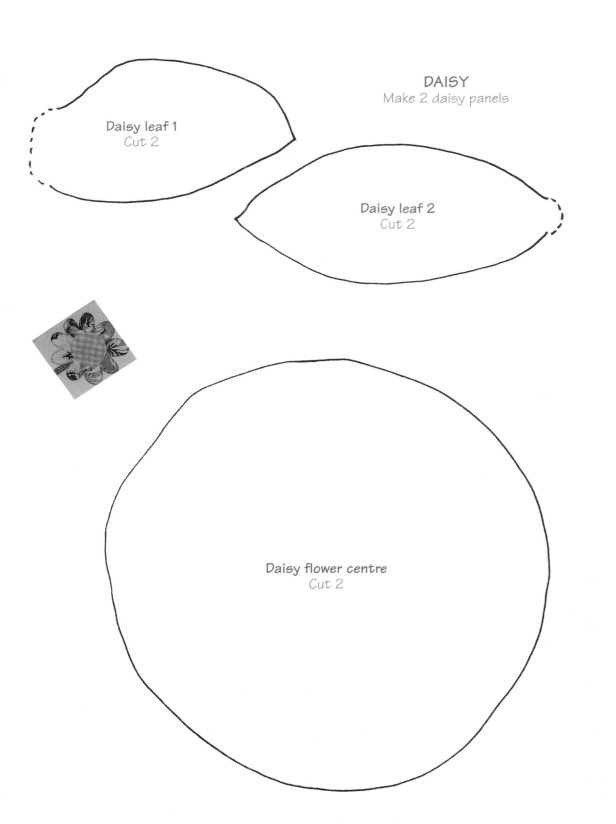

DAISY
Make 2 daisy panels

Daisy leaf 1
Cut 2

Daisy leaf 2
Cut 2

Daisy flower centre
Cut 2

Daisy stem width *Adjust length as needed.* Cut 2

DAFFODIL
Make 3 daffodil panels

Daffodil petals
Cut 3

Daffodil leaf shape Adjust length as
needed. Cut 3 long and 3 short leaves

Daffodil flower centre
Cut 3

Daffodil stem width Adjust length as needed. Cut 3

piece from each fabric. Take care to cut any big appliqué pieces first if you want them from particular fabrics, so that you don't find yourself with fabric pieces too small for the larger shapes.

From these fabrics, cut the following:

A total of sixteen 4⅞ inch squares for the pinwheels. Cut these squares in lots of two from each fabric. Cut the squares once on the diagonal to yield thirty-two half-square triangles.

A total of forty-four 4½ inch squares for the four-patches.

Appliqué flowers and hearts as described below. Please take the time to read the appliqué instructions before cutting.

FROM EACH OF THE SIX BACKGROUND FABRICS, CUT:

One piece 9 x 25 inches.

One piece 9 x 17 inches.

These pieces are larger than you need, but you can trim them back to the correct size after working the appliqué. This will allow for fraying while you hand stitch.

Appliqué

Vliesofix has a paper side, which is smooth, and a webbing side, which is rough. Choose a flower to begin with, and trace the components of the flower onto the paper side of the Vliesofix. Cut these shapes out roughly using paper scissors. Next choose a fabric for the stem, grass, petals and flower centre. Using a hot iron, iron the roughly cut Vliesofix shapes onto

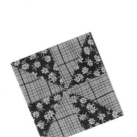

the back of the fabrics, with the webbing side down. It is vital that the webbing side is down, or the shape will stick to your iron.

Next, using sharp fabric scissors, cut the shapes out of the fabric along the pencil line. Peel the paper off the fabric, leaving the webbing stuck to the back of the fabric.

Turn the shapes right side up and position them onto your background piece. Ensure you have chosen the right sized background piece for the type of flower; see the table below. Now iron the pieces down. They should now be stuck to the background panel.

ALERT! *Note carefully which piece of the flower should be laid down first; for example, the top of the stem should be* under *the head of the flower, and the bottom* under *the grass. The dotted lines on the template pieces indicate what portion should go under another piece.*

If you are hand appliquéing, choose an embroidery thread to match or contrast, whichever appeals to you, with the fabric you have used. Using two strands of thread, blanket stitch around all raw edges of the appliqué pieces (any edges that are underneath another shape do not need to be stitched; any edges that are showing do).

If you are appliquéing by machine, set your blanket stitch to a width of 1.5 and a length of 2. Try the stitch out on a piece of scrap to make sure you are happy with the result, then stitch around the shapes as above.

Repeat with all the appliqué shapes until all the panels are complete.

FLOWER TYPES

Make flower appliqué panels as follows:

Daffodil	9 x 17 inch piece	make 3
Tulip	9 x 17 inch piece	make 3
Gerberas	9 x 25 inch piece	make 2
Hearts	9 x 25 inch piece	make 2
Daisy	9 x 25 inch piece	make 2
Border Sunflower	8½ inch squares of white	make 10

Piecing

PINWHEELS

Piece together two contrasting half-square triangles along the bias edge, until you have 32 pairs. Iron the seams to one side and clip the 'ears' off the triangles. Taking care to position the fabrics so that the pinwheel pattern is formed (see photograph at left), sew two squares together and press the seams to one side. Repeat until you have 16 of these units.

Taking care to match the corners and the centre seam, piece two units together to form a pinwheel. You should have eight pinwheels, each measuring 8½ inches square.

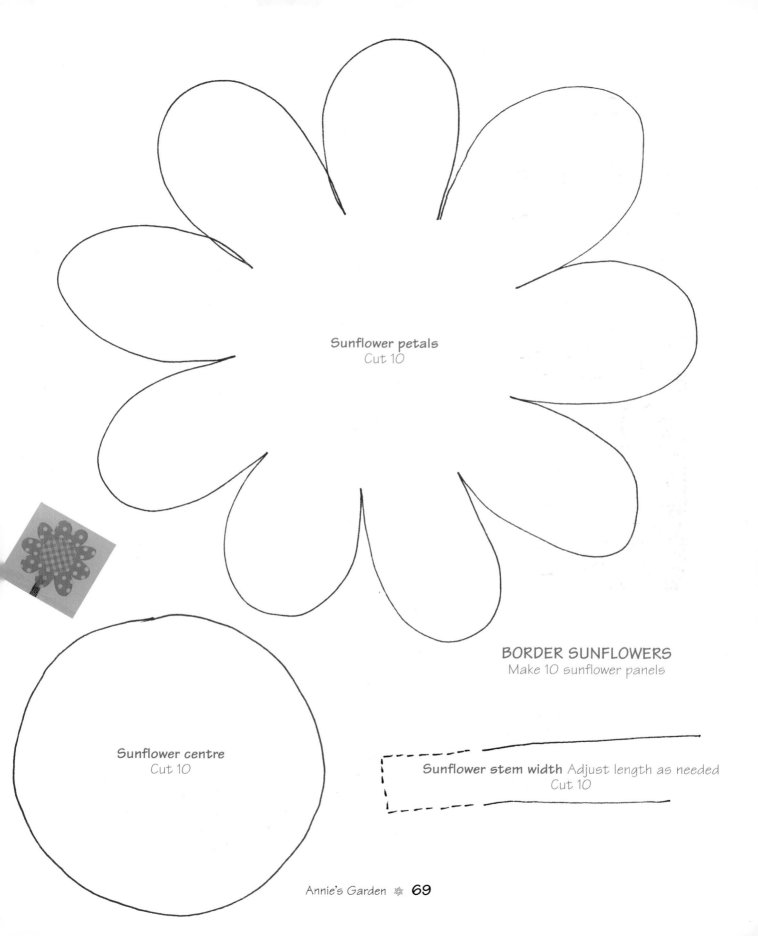

Sunflower petals
Cut 10

Sunflower centre
Cut 10

BORDER SUNFLOWERS
Make 10 sunflower panels

Sunflower stem width Adjust length as needed
Cut 10

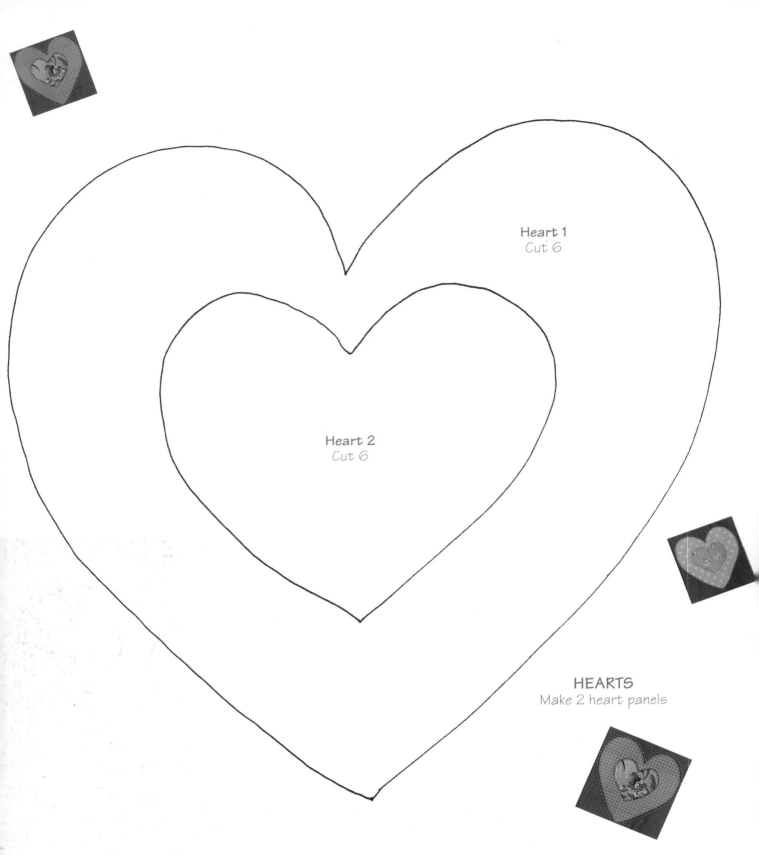

Heart 1
Cut 6

Heart 2
Cut 6

HEARTS
Make 2 heart panels

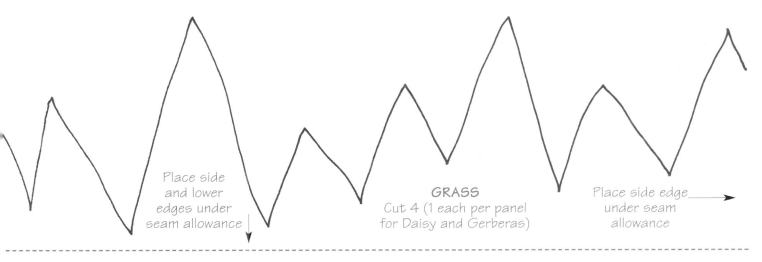

Place side
and lower
edges under
seam allowance ↓

GRASS
Cut 4 (1 each per panel
for Daisy and Gerberas)

Place side edge⟶
under seam
allowance

FOUR-PATCHES

Piece together white squares and patterned squares into pairs. Piece these pairs together, alternating the white and patterned squares, to form a four-patch. You should have 22 four-patches.

Construction

Piece together the four-patch units in a vertical strip of ten blocks. Repeat with ten of the remaining blocks. You should have two blocks left over.

Trim the appliquéd blocks back to their correct sizes; the smaller blocks should be 8½ x 16½ inches, and the larger 8½ x 24½ inches. Ensure that the appliquéd flower is centred on the trimmed block.

Using the photograph on page 75 as a guide for placement, stitch the appliqué blocks together in a vertical strip as follows:

ROW 1	ROW 2	ROW 3
Gerberas	Tulip	Hearts
Daffodil	Daisy	Tulip
Hearts	Daffodil	Daisy
Tulip	Gerberas	Daffodil

Press the rows carefully.

Next, stitch Row 1 to a row of four-patches, Row 2 to the other side, then another row of four-patches, then finish with Row 3. This completes the centre panel of the quilt.

Press the centre panel carefully and measure. Your panel should measure 40½ x 80½ inches. Trim to fit if it does not.

Remove the selvedges from the 2½ inch strips of red spot fabric. Stitch two together end to end to make a long strip, and trim to measure 80½ x 2½ inches. Repeat to make one more long strip.

Fold the quilt in half along its length to find the centre of one edge and finger-press a crease. Do the same to one of the red inner border strips. Pin, right sides together, at the centre marks, then pin the ends. Now pin

Gerbera 1
Petals
Cut 2

all along the sides, gently easing as necessary. This will ensure the borders will not buckle your quilt top. Stitch, then repeat with the other red strip.

To form the outer border, stitch the pinwheels and sunflower squares together, alternating them, beginning and ending with a pinwheel, and adding a four patch in the centre of the row. There should be ten blocks to a strip. Repeat to form the other border and attach as for the inner border strip. Press. Your quilt top is now complete. Press it carefully.

Backing, quilting and binding

Measure the completed quilt top and cut backing fabric to fit, allowing a little extra, and piecing if necessary to obtain the correct size.

See pages 192–197 for instructions on finishing.

The pictured example was quilted using light pink perle cotton No 8. The four-patch blocks were quilted in a cross hatch pattern, and the flowers were outline quilted.

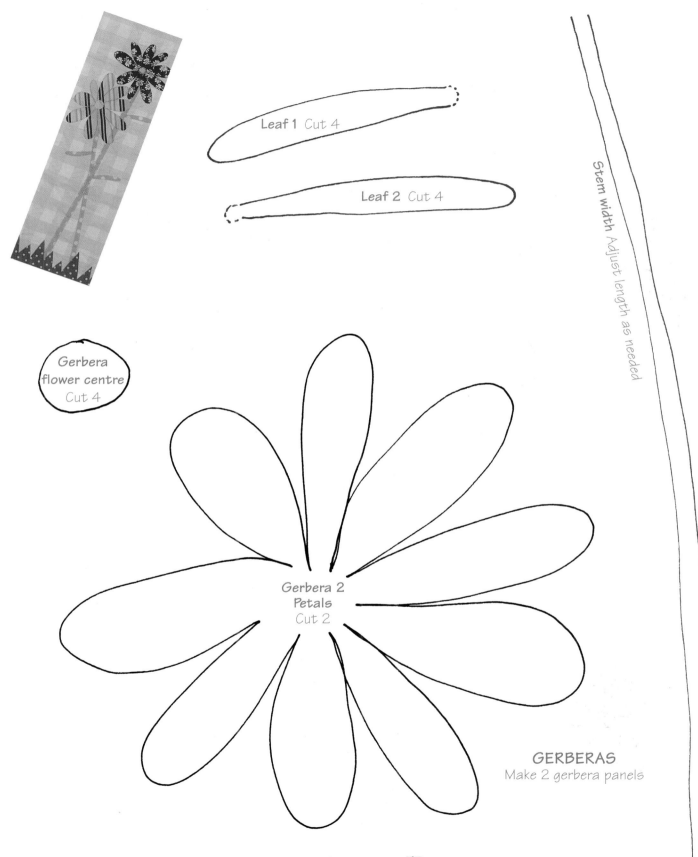

Leaf 1 Cut 4

Leaf 2 Cut 4

Stem width Adjust length as needed

Gerbera
flower centre
Cut 4

Gerbera 2
Petals
Cut 2

GERBERAS
Make 2 gerbera panels

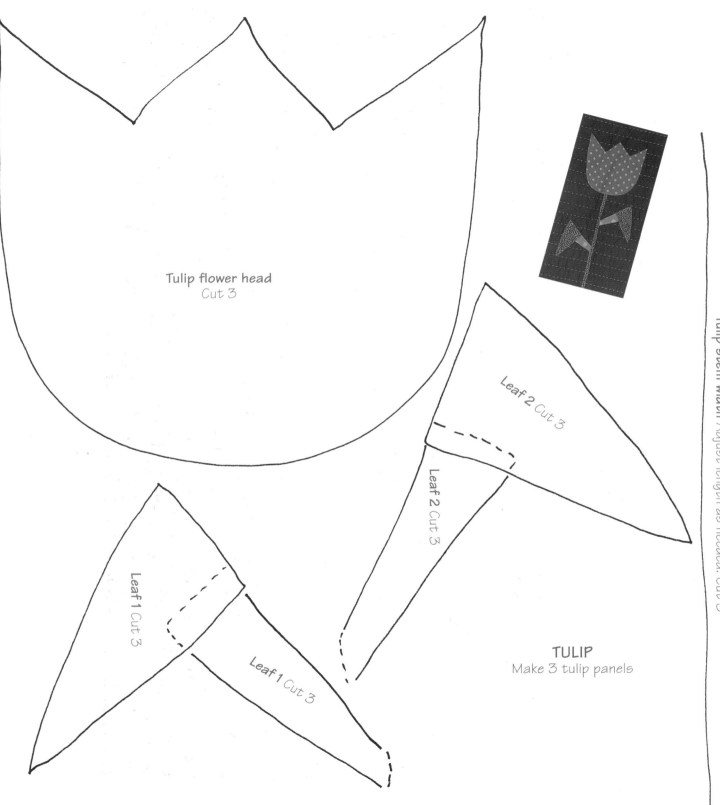

Tulip flower head
Cut 3

Leaf 2 Cut 3

Leaf 2 Cut 3

Leaf 1 Cut 3

Leaf 1 Cut 3

Tulip stem width Adjust length as needed. Cut 3

TULIP
Make 3 tulip panels

Rocket Man

Kathy Doughty   INTERMEDIATE

THE IDEA

Okay, we used a panel here but you could just as easily get your young astronaut to use fabric pens and draw his own rocket or astronaut!

A variety of starred and spotted navy fabrics give an idea of the night sky, and as for the coloured stars themselves … well, I literally dumped my scrap bucket on the floor, and separated the bits into piles of warm and cool colours. From there I hardly even looked as I took star points from alternating piles.

To emphasise the star tracks, freewheeling lines were hand quilted in white thread.

Finished quilt size

Cot quilt, 90 x 137 cm (36 x 54½ inches)

Materials and tools

1 Prints Charming rocket panel measuring 26 x 39 cm (10½ x 15⅓ inches), or use your own panel, photo transfer or appliqué

2.25 m (2½ yards) navy star and/or spot fabrics (the quilt pictured used seven different fabrics)

1 m (40 inches) scrap pieces in a mixture of cool and warm colours

40 cm (16 inches) binding fabric

1.5 m (60 inches) backing fabric

1.2 x 1.5 m (47 x 60 inch) piece cotton wadding

Quarter-inch ruler

2B pencil and sharpener, or chalk

Masking tape

Perle cotton No 8 in white and navy

NOTE: *It is recommended that all fabrics be 100 percent cotton, and be ironed. Requirements are based on fabric 112 cm (44 inches) wide. Unless otherwise stated, all seam allowances are ¼ inch throughout. Colour test any dark fabrics that you are using (see page 177); if they run, wash them before cutting.*

Please read all instructions before starting.

Cutting

All fabrics are strip cut across the width of the fabric, from selvedge to fold (cut off all selvedges first).

FROM THE NAVY STAR AND/OR SPOT FABRICS, CUT:

Five strips 6½ inches wide, then cross cut into 26 squares. Set 10 aside.

Twelve strips 2½ inches wide. Cross cut these into 198 squares.

Two strips 2 inches wide x 15½ inches long.

Two strips 1½ inches wide x 12½ inches long.

FROM THE BINDING FABRIC, cut five strips 2½ inches wide.

TRIM THE ROCKET PANEL to 10½ x 15½ inches.

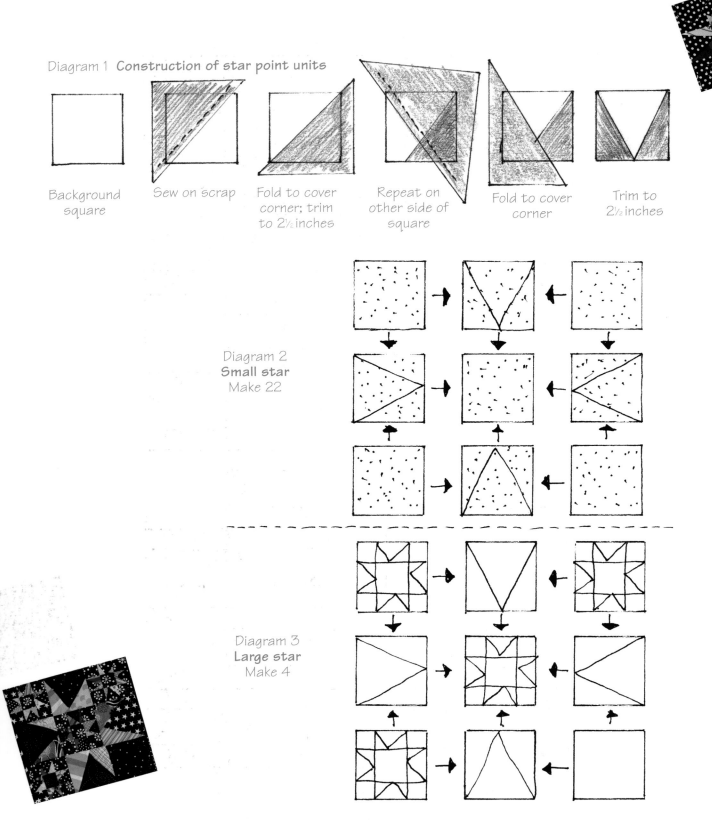

Diagram 1 **Construction of star point units**

Background square

Sew on scrap

Fold to cover corner; trim to 2½ inches

Repeat on other side of square

Fold to cover corner

Trim to 2½ inches

Diagram 2
Small star
Make 22

Diagram 3
Large star
Make 4

Diagram 4 **Quilt construction**

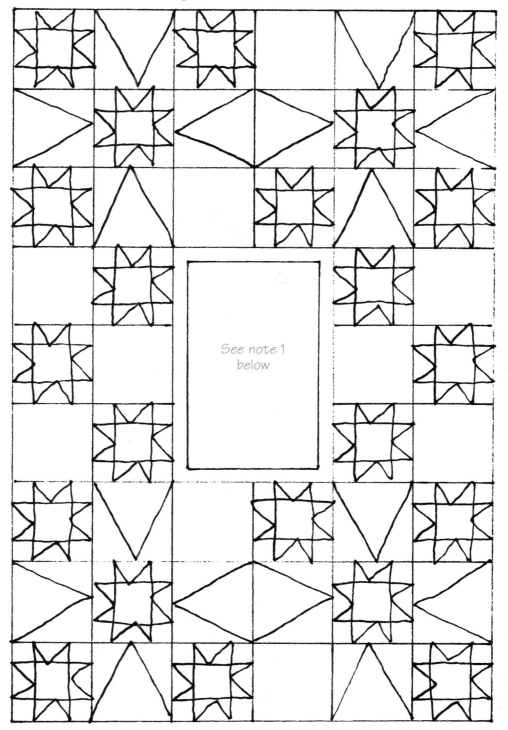

See note 1
below

See
note 2
below

1. Because the rocket panels are hand screen printed, they may vary a litle in size. If your rocket is too large for
   the central rectangle, omit the small surrounding border.
2. Remember that your stars are meant to be wonky, not regular like the ones drawn here.

Sewing

The star blocks are made using the same method regardless of their size.

Separate the scrap pieces into cool and warm colours. Any scraps can be used, but they should be bigger than the space you need to cover to allow for the seam allowance. Study the photograph opposite; note that the star points vary in size and angle, with some running from the corner of the background fabric and others starting part way down from the corners. This randomness gives visual texture and movement to the quilt.

Lay a navy square face up and place a scrap fabric face down on top. Sew a diagonal seam through both layers (see Diagram 1 on page 78).

Fold the top layer back and press flat. Trim the scrap fabric and square it off to the original size of the navy square. Repeat the process, with the diagonal seam going toward the opposite corner as shown in the diagram. You have now completed one star point unit.

Make eighty-eight 2½ inch star point units in this manner.

Make sixteen 6½ inch star point units in the same manner.

To make the small star blocks, lay out four 2½ inch star point units and five plain 2½ inch navy star squares to form a star (see Diagram 2 on page 78). Match the seams and sew together. Make 22 small star blocks in this manner.

To make the large star blocks, lay out four small star blocks, four 6½ inch star point units and one 6½ inch navy square to make a nine-patch (see Diagram 3 on page 78). The centre of each large square is a small star block, and each large star has one plain corner square. Make 4.

To make the units that border the rocket panel, sew together small star blocks and 6½ inch navy star squares in pairs, then join the pairs in three rows of two, alternating the placement of stars and plain blocks in each row as shown in the photograph opposite.

To the sides of the rocket panel, sew the 15½ inch navy print strips, if needed (see the note on page 79). To the top and bottom of this unit, if needed, sew the 12½ inch navy print strips.

Sew all the components together as shown in Diagram 4 on page 79. Your quilt top is now complete. Press the quilt top carefully.

Backing, quilting and binding

When the top is complete, measure your backing fabric and cut to fit.

See pages 192–197 for instructions on finishing.

The pictured example was quilted using continuous freehand quilting to make white lines flowing through the galaxy and the navy shadow stars. To do this, make a chalk line through the squares and follow it using white perle cotton and about five stitches to the inch. To reinforce the design of the rocket, quilt around the dark lines.

The 'Burbs

Sarah Fielke   INTERMEDIATE

THE IDEA

The one thing to remember about this quilt is … let yourself go! This quilt is a recipe, not a pattern. There are no set sizes for the dolls or houses, so there is no set size for the quilt. Make some of your dolls and houses first, then pin them up on a sheet of flannel or lay them out on the floor until you are happy with the result. If you want more, make more! When you are happy, join them up. There are no rules here — just cut, sew and enjoy! This quilt is a good project for using up scraps.

The inspiration for this quilt came from *Collaborative Quilting*, by Freddie Moran and Gwen Marston, and the Cut Loose Quilters.

Finished quilt size

Wall hanging or throw — whatever! The pictured example is 120 x 140 cm (47 x 55 inches), therefore the material requirements are based on a quilt of approximately that size.

Due to the haphazard nature of construction, the following material requirements are approximate.

Materials and tools

1.5 m (60 inches) white floral for linking squares
1.5 m (60 inches) in total of different pinks for doll backgrounds
1 m (40 inches) large pink stripe or similar for house backgrounds
20 cm (8 inches) cream for dolls' faces and hands
40 cm (16 inches) brown for roofs and dolls' legs, or use scraps
Scraps of lots of different fabrics of all colours, from 5 cm (2 inches) square to 13 cm (5 inches) square, for hats, windows, doors and daisies in the gardens and borders
1 m (40 inches) multicoloured stripe for border
50 cm (20 inches) brown fabric for inner border and binding
2.4 m (95 inches) backing fabric
Cotton wadding at least 140 x 160 cm (55 x 64 inches)
Perle cotton No 8 in chocolate brown for quilting
Assorted buttons, ric-rac, trim and whatever else you might like to jazz up your dollies with. Please be mindful that if the quilt is for a small child, buttons are not advised

NOTE: *It is recommended that all fabrics be 100 percent cotton, and be ironed. Requirements are based on fabric 112 cm (44 inches) wide. Unless otherwise stated, all seam allowances are ¼ inch throughout. Colour test any dark fabrics that you are using (see page 177); if they run, wash them before cutting.*

Please read all instructions before starting.

Making dolls

In this quilt there are several sizes of dolls. In fact, no two of them are the same size. I didn't cut a specific size skirt or anything else, I just took pieces and chopped bits off and went from there. If you want a more definite recipe, though, do the following:

FOR A SMALL DOLLY, CUT:
One 4 inch square from 'dress' fabric
One 4 x 1 inch strip from 'dress' fabric
Two 2½ x 4½ inch pieces from the pink background

Diagram 1 **Doll construction**

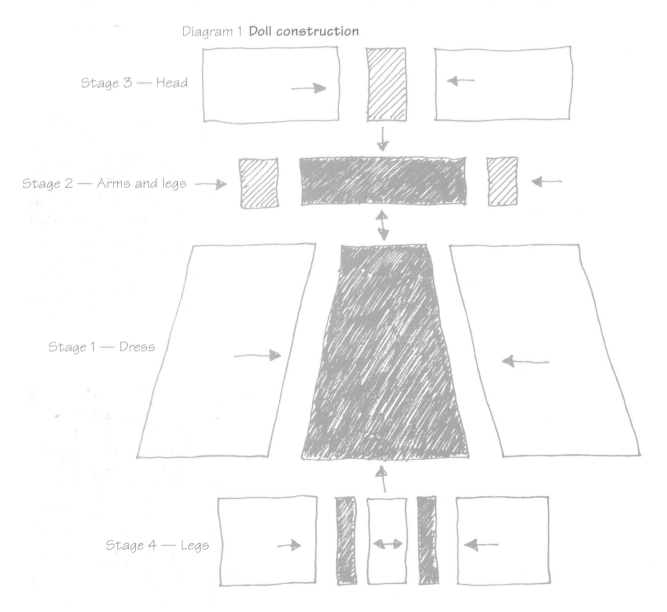

Two 3 x 1½ inch pieces from the pink background

Two pieces 2 x 1½ inches and one piece 1 x 1½ inches from the pink background

One 1½ inch square and two pieces 1 x 1½ inches from cream 'face' fabric

Two pieces 1 x 1½ inches from the brown fabric for legs.

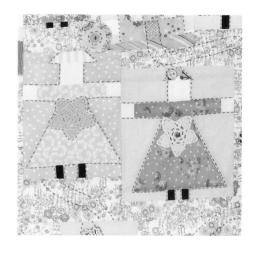

SEWING DOLLS

1 Begin by finding the centre of your dress fabric 4 inch square by folding it in half and finger pressing a line at the top. Bearing in mind that this is the centre of the dolly, place one pink background 2½ x 4½ inch piece randomly and at an angle onto the dolly's dress about 1 inch from the centre mark, right sides together.

2 Sew a ¼ inch seam along the pink fabric and trim off the excess dress fabric.

3 Repeat on the other side of the square. Do not be concerned that the pieces are not exactly the same, or worry too much about measuring. Press the seams open toward the background fabric. See Stage 1 of the diagram opposite.

4 Trim the top and bottom edges flat with the original 4 inch square. Do not trim the sides yet. This piece forms the doll's dress.

5 Next, sew a 1 x 1½ inch cream rectangle to either end of the 4 x 1 inch piece of dress fabric and press the seam toward the dress fabric. See Stage 2 of the diagram. This piece forms your arms and hands. Make sure it is shorter than the width of your skirt/background piece, otherwise when you come to trim the unit you will cut off her hands!

6 Take the remaining piece of cream fabric and piece a 1½ inch strip of background fabric to either side. See Stage 3 of the diagram. This is the doll's head.

7 For the legs, piece a strip as follows — 2 x 1½ inch piece pink background, leg, 1 x 1½ inch piece pink, leg, 2 x 1½ inch piece pink. Press the seams toward the legs. See Stage 4 of the diagram.

8 Before you join your doll together, consider what she might have sewn to her dress. If you plan to use trim or add an apron, now is the time to do it. To add trim such as ric-rac along the top or bottom edge of the dress, tack it on now by hand. When you come to sew the pieces together, the edge you tacked will be caught neatly in the seam.

To add an apron, cut two U-shaped pieces, larger than the finished size you want, from contrasting fabric. Sew them together around the U, leaving the straight edge open. Clip around the curves with small sharp scissors and turn the apron through. Iron the seam flat, then tack the flat edge of the apron to the dress at the top and continue as before.

I recommend not adding buttons and bulkier embellishments until later, as it makes it difficult to iron and sew the dolls together.

9 Finger-press the centre mark into the hands piece, the head piece and the leg piece. Line up all the centre marks and sew your doll together. She should look like the photograph at left (minus the hat).

10 Trim the piece to be square.

MAKING LARGE DOLLS

Repeat the above steps, but use larger measurements. For example, start with a 6 inch square for the dress, cut 6½ x 4½ inch pieces for the backgrounds, 6 x 2 inch pieces for the arms and 3½ x 2 inch head strips. My only recommendation is that the legs should not be cut wider than 1½ inches, otherwise they will be very stumpy! Also, the head should not get too big; the largest head I cut was 2 inches square.

Once you have made one dolly, you will see that it doesn't really matter what size you cut your pieces, so long as the background is big enough to cover the sides of the dress square and that the arm, leg and head pieces are long enough to trim back if you need to when the doll is all together. Experiment with different sizes — try tall dollies and short, fat dollies. Don't forget that wonky dollies are just as much fun as straight ones! Having many different shapes and sizes, and a few that aren't perfect, is what makes the quilt fun.

ADDING THE DOLL'S HAT

You may have noticed that your doll has no hat. Any well-dressed suburban lady wears a hat to go out, and there are a few ways to make her one.

Hat one is made by sewing an extra strip the same dimensions as your head strip, but with a coloured square where the head should be. This will give your lady a square hat. You can then sew a button on to make it a pillbox, or a piece of ribbon or ric-rac for a brim. You can vary this hat by making it tall and thin, or short and flat.

Hat two is a triangular hat, which is made by cutting a triangle of any shape that is at least ½ inch wider at the base than the dolly's head. Cut the same angle from either side of a background strip and piece the triangle in. The background strip *must* be at least ½ inch wider than the triangle's height to allow for seams.

Your last option is to sew a plain strip above the doll's head, then add a hat by hand. This could be a yo-yo (suffolk puff), a huge button, a piece of felt or anything else you can think of. This is the easiest way to add a hat.

Making houses

For a medium-sized, square house, cut the following:

Two 2½ inch square pieces from the 'house' fabric

One 1½ x 5½ inch strip from the 'house' fabric

One 1½ x 3 inch and two 2½ x 1½ inch pieces from the 'house' fabric

One 2½ x 1½ inch piece for the door

Two 1½ inch square pieces for windows

One strip 3 inches wide x length of fabric from the pink and white
background stripe

Piece of green fabric for grass.

SEWING HOUSES

1 Sew the two 2½ inch squares to either side of the door.

2 Sew a 2½ x 1½ inch piece to either side of the windows, and the 1½ x
3 inch piece in between.

3 Join these three strips together and trim the sides level with each other.
If you want your house to be on a bit of a lean, you can trim the sides
at an angle. See Stage 1 of the diagram on page 88.

4 Sew the 3 inch stripe strip to the side of the house, then trim the end
off level with the bottom of the house. Repeat with the other side, and
trim all the ends off level. See Stage 2 of the diagram on page 88.

5 Next, consider your grass. If you want your house to be on a hill, trim
the bottom edge off at a slight angle. Sew a strip of grass fabric to the
bottom edge. See Stage 3 of the diagram on page 88.

6 For a roof, you have a few options. For a pitched roof, you can cut a
large triangle, sew the striped fabric to either side at an angle then trim.
Remember to leave enough fabric at the point for the seam allowance.
For a flat roof, cut a strip of the brown fabric and cut the ends at an
angle. Piece the striped fabric to either end, trim to make a level strip
and add another strip of striped fabric above for sky. Do not be
concerned about running the stripe in any one direction; the stripe
actually looks better pieced at all different angles.

7 Join all the roof to the rest of the house and trim the block to be level.

8 Try houses of all different shapes and sizes. The only house rule to stick
to is that the door should be rectangular in order to look like a door.
Sounds obvious, but believe me it's important!

Construction

The pictured quilt has 11 houses and 13 dolls. When you think you are
approaching an appropriate amount of dollies and houses (or are just
getting sick of making them!), pin them to a piece of pellon or flannel
hung on the wall until you are happy with where they sit. It is best to use
something that you can roll up and put away in between piecing, as you
don't want to forget where you had things placed. Remember that they do
not have to sit in rows, but can be placed randomly. Make sure you are
happy with the colour placement and the arrangement of light and dark
dresses etc. Step back and have a good long look. Do you need more
houses? More dollies? Are there too many, so that they need to be spread

Diagram 2 **House construction**

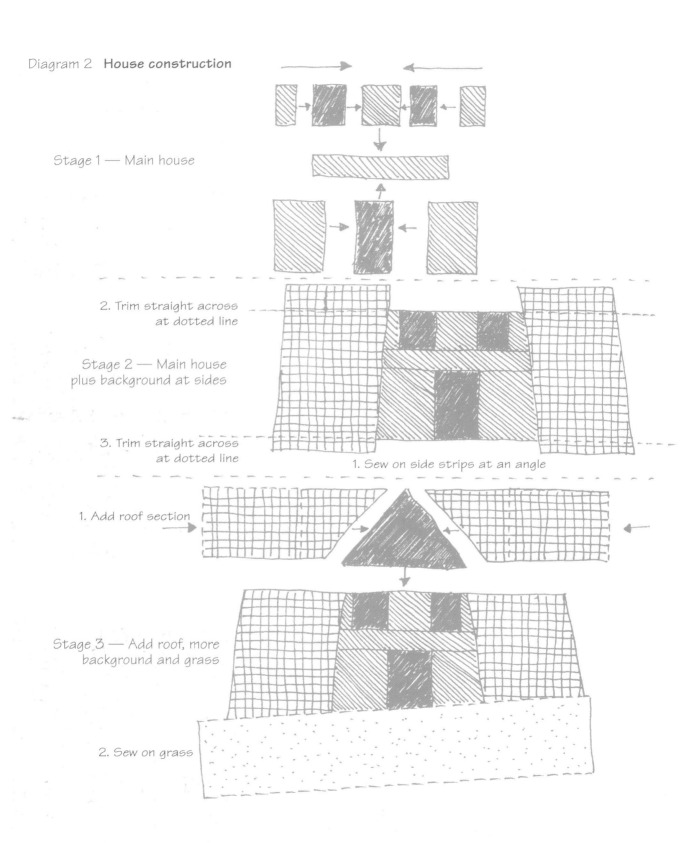

Stage 1 — Main house

2. Trim straight across
   at dotted line

Stage 2 — Main house
plus background at sides

3. Trim straight across
   at dotted line

1. Sew on side strips at an angle

1. Add roof section

Stage 3 — Add roof, more
background and grass

2. Sew on grass

out? Is the quilt too small, or too big? Don't forget that you will add a border, which will make your quilt larger. There is no right answer here — if you like your composition and it looks right to you, then it's perfect!

When you have decided on your placement, start the construction of the top.

First, cut some strips of varying widths from your background fabric — some 3 inches wide, some 4 inches, even some 5 inches if you have large gaps between your blocks. Look carefully at the dolls and try to see where you can sew pieces together without using an L-shaped seam. Break the top down into sections, and work on piecing one section at a time.

Using a ¼ inch seam allowance, piece the blocks together using the different sized strips. Estimate the distance between the blocks, sew the strip on, then trim it off until it fits. Don't worry about measuring, just go for it and you will find it comes together.

Continue in this manner until you have pieced all the sections, then join your sections together. Your centre panel is now complete.

Borders

Measure your centre panel and trim the edges if they are not square. Press the entire centre panel carefully.

From the border fabric, cut strips 6 inches wide. If your quilt is roughly the same size as the pictured one, you will need five strips. Measure the width of the quilt through the centre and cut two strips to this length. Find the centre of one strip and the centre of the top edge of the quilt and finger-press a crease. Match these points and pin. Next pin the ends, then pin in between. This quilt is made with lots of different bias, so this step is very important to ensure your border doesn't stretch out of shape. Sew, then repeat with the bottom of the quilt.

Measure the quilt from top to bottom through the middle and cut two strips to this size. You may have to join pieces from the fifth strip to make the strips long enough. Repeat as above to attach the side borders.

Decoration

Now is the time to embellish your dollies. You can sew buttons, trims, patches and beads onto their dresses to dress them up. Use your imagination to make each dolly an individual.

Backing, quilting and binding

When the top is complete, measure your backing fabric and cut to fit, allowing a little extra, and piecing it if necessary to get the right size.

Refer to pages 192–197 for instructions on finishing.

The pictured example was quilted using chocolate brown perle cotton to outline the dollies and houses, and to quilt garden paths for the houses.

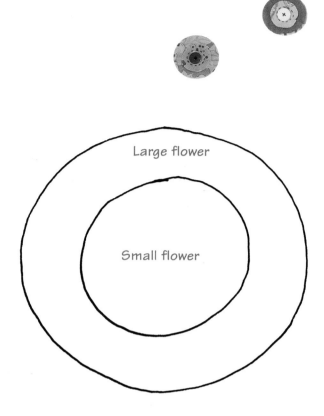

Large flower

Small flower

Garden borders

You thought you were all done! Now your houses need gardens. Begin by cutting ten or twelve large and small circles from assorted fabrics, using the templates above; or you can trace around different sized glasses or cups if you prefer. Lay the small flowers on top of the large, and arrange them over the quilt top in the gardens of the houses and in the sashing pieces. If you need more flowers, cut more. Pin them in place when you are happy so you don't forget where they go. Cut some more and do the same with the border. Scatter the flowers randomly and use lots of different fabrics for a scrappy look.

When you like your garden, sew a button through all three layers of the quilt, and sew a running stitch around the smaller circle, about ¼ inch in from the edge. This can act as quilting and also will attach the flower. When the flower is sewn on, use small sharp scissors to clip both circles about ¼ inch apart all the way around, taking care not to clip the quilt or the running stitches.

OK, now you're done. Enjoy your quilt ... and good job!

Holiday Morning

Kathy Doughty

INTERMEDIATE

THE IDEA

This quilt is all about the image of looking out of a window at singing birds. The colours I chose were reds, pinks, hot greens and purples but also some yellows — anything goes, really. It doesn't take much fabric to make the birds, and they work best if done in tone-on-tone fabrics or small prints, with contrasting wings.

A new technique in appliqué using foil, and a fashionable trend to use simple bird shapes, made this quilt sing. It was quilted while enjoying quiet mornings at the beach on holiday, hence the name.

Finished quilt size
Wall hanging, 92 x 112 cm (36 x 44 inches)
Finished block size: 13 x 16¾ inches including seam allowance

Materials and tools
1.3 m (52 inches) white fabric for background
75 cm (30 inches) in total of 2–3 colours for border
10 cm (4 inches) of each of four colours for the birds and flowers
75 cm (30 inches) white fabric for border
15 cm (6 inches) of each of four greens for border corners and leaves
25 cm (10 inches) brown pin-dot fabric for stems
Thin scrap of grey fabric at least 50 cm (20 inches) long, for telegraph line
70 cm (30 inches) small brown print fabric for the frames and binding
2.4 m (95 inches) backing fabric
1 x 1.5 m (40 x 60 inch) piece cotton wadding
Rotary cutter, ruler and mat
Quarter-square ruler and half-square ruler (optional)
Neutral cotton thread for piecing
2–3 balls perle cotton for quilting (for accents)
White quilting cotton (for background)
Kitchen foil and cardboard (card stock) for appliqué

NOTE: *It is recommended that all fabrics be 100 percent cotton, and be ironed. Requirements are based on fabric 112 cm (44 inches) wide. Unless otherwise stated, all seam allowances are ¼ inch throughout. Colour test any dark fabrics that you are using (see page 177); if they run, wash them before cutting.*

The instructions read the way they do to allow for the bias difference between half-square and quarter-square triangles.

Preparation
Use the templates provided to cut out the appliqué shapes. To do this, trace the shapes onto cardboard using a sharp 2B pencil and cut out. Each template can be used several times; discard once the edges become worn.

Diagram 1 **Panel background, branches**

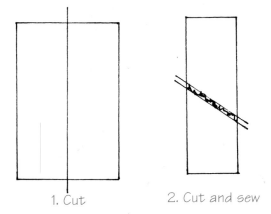

1. Cut   2. Cut and sew

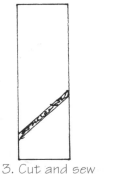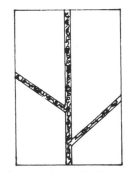

3. Cut and sew   4. Join both halves
Finished 12 x 16¼ inches

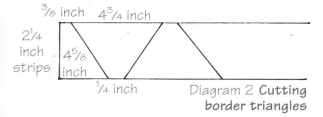

3/8 inch   4¾ inch

2¼ inch strips   4⅝ inch

¼ inch   Diagram 2 **Cutting border triangles**

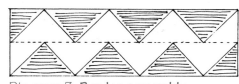

Diagram 3 **Border assembly**

Cutting

All fabrics are strip cut across the width of the fabric, from selvedge to fold; cut off all selvedges first. Please read through the directions before starting. The cutting instructions are labelled alphabetically, but cut the largest pieces first and use the remaining bits to cut the smaller strips.

NOTE: *Some instructions are written for use with the half-square and quarter-square rulers. If you are not using these rulers, disregard these instructions so as not to confuse yourself.*

FROM THE BACKGROUND FABRIC, cut four panels 25 x 20 inches. (Later, once the branch pieces and the appliquéd shapes are added, these will be trimmed back to 13 x 16¾ inches.)

FROM THE FRAME AND BINDING FABRIC, CUT:
Three strips 1½ inches wide. Cross cut these into six strips 16¾ inches long for the frames.
Three strips 1¾ inches wide. Trim these to 28½ inches long for the frames.
Five strips 2½ inches wide for the binding.

FROM THE BRANCH FABRIC, cut 10–12 strips of brown fabric 1–2 inches wide by up to 25 inches long (vary the widths of the strips to give thinner and thicker branches, as shown in the photo on page 97).

FROM THE BIRD, FLOWER AND LEAF FABRICS:
Use the cardboard templates to mark the shapes onto the reverse of the fabric, then cut out, allowing a scant ¼ inch seam allowance. At this point it is recommended that you also cut foil pieces just bigger than the fabric. Place the foil on the ironing board, then the fabric face down and the cardboard templates on top. Use the foil to gently fold the fabric around the smooth edges of the cardboard and press for a few seconds. The foil will press a crease around the curved edges that will make it easy to needle-turn the shapes onto the background.
The same shape is used to cut the flower petals, birds' wings and leaves. Cut forty leaves, ten wings and six flower petals.
Cut ten bird bodies, four small circles and three large circles.

FROM THE COLOURED BORDER FABRICS:
If you are using the quarter-square and half-square rulers, cut six strips 2¼ inches wide. Use the quarter-square ruler to cut 60 quarter-square triangles.
Cut eight half-square triangles from one of the 2¼ inch strips using the half-square ruler, or cut them from the ends of the strips used above.
If you are not using the quarter-square and half-square rulers, cut fifteen 4¾ inch squares and cross cut them on both diagonals to make four triangles per square. Then cut four 2⅞ inch squares and cross cut on one diagonal for the half-square triangles. Do this in both white border fabric and in the coloured fabrics.

FROM THE REMAINING GREEN FABRICS, cut four 4 inch squares for the corners.

FROM THE WHITE BORDER FABRIC, CUT:

Six strips 2¼ inches wide. Following the instructions above, cross cut these on both diagonals to give 60 quarter-square triangles.

Eight half-square triangles from one 2¼ inch strip using the half-square ruler, or cut them from the ends of the strips from above.

Sewing

ZIGZAG BORDER

Sew the border together first by matching the diagonal sides of the quarter-square triangles in pairs of white and coloured fabrics. Press the seams toward the coloured fabrics.

Sew nine pairs together into four long strips. End two of these with a white half-square triangle. Repeat the same process, only this time end with the coloured half-square triangle.

Match the points of the white quarter-square triangles down the length of the strip and pin together, then sew the strips to form the side border. Repeat for the other side.

For the top and bottom border, repeat the process with seven sets of pairs. Refer to the photograph on page 97 if you get confused.

MAIN BLOCKS

Start with the four background rectangles. One at a time, cut three of them along the length, making one or more of the cuts at a slight angle if you wish. Make sure to note which side is which and, referring to the diagrams, cut each piece diagonally and at an angle across the width to allow for insertion of the branch strips.

Match your branch strips to the horizontal cuts and sew together as shown in Diagram 1. Do both horizontal cuts first and then reassemble them by inserting a branch into the long vertical cut. Your blocks need not look exactly like the ones pictured. Have a play and have fun doing this.

When the branches are complete, lay out your bird and flower shapes and needle-turn appliqué them in place (see page 189). You can copy the designs in the photo or try something different. Once you get the hang of the shapes, you can add more birds or have them fly away. It's that easy!

Backstitch the birds' beaks and legs using brown stranded cotton.

Trim the four appliquéd panels to the correct size of 13 x 16¾ inches.

When the four main panels are finished, join two panels and three 16¾ inch framing strips, alternating them, and beginning and ending with a framing strip. You should have a strip that reads thus: frame, panel, frame, panel, frame.

Make another strip the same.

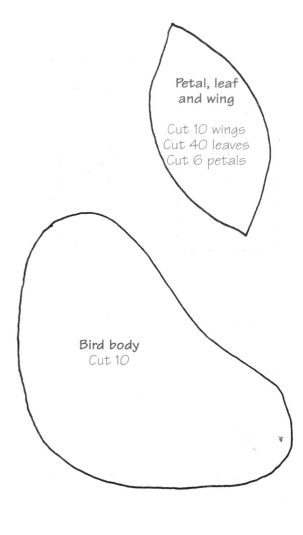

Petal, leaf and wing

Cut 10 wings
Cut 40 leaves
Cut 6 petals

Bird body
Cut 10

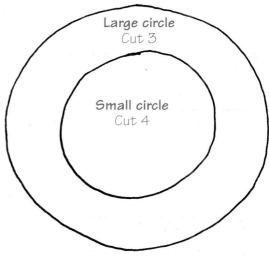

Large circle
Cut 3

Small circle
Cut 4

Sew these two strips together with a long framing strip in the middle, then add the other long framing strips to the top and the bottom. To get a good result, remember to find the middle of the pieces first and finger-press a crease. Match these points and pin, then match and pin the ends, then pin all along the sides, gently easing as necessary.

Borders

When the frames are complete, add the zigzag borders in the same manner. Attach the side borders first. Add the 4 inch green squares to both ends of the top and bottom borders. Match the centre points and the ends, then pin all the way along, easing as necessary, then sew together.

The quilt top is now complete. Press the entire quilt top carefully.

Backing, quilting and binding

Measure your backing fabric and cut it to fit, allowing a little extra.

Refer to pages 192–197 for instructions on finishing.

The pictured example was quilted with white quilting cotton on the background. I used a chalk pencil and drew flower shapes in the big white areas. Then to give it a bit of texture I drew radiating lines from the birds' beaks and from the corners of the blocks. In addition I outlined the various shapes with perle cotton in colours to match them.

Summer Sunshine

Sarah Fielke

INTERMEDIATE

THE IDEA

My inspiration for this quilt was an antique quilt I love. The block is beautiful and symmetrical, but the original is stitched with black thread and the colours are duller. I used brighter 1930s reproduction prints in keeping with the history of the original, but used the stripes and the yellow border to give a boost of modern-day sunshine. You could make your flowers darker, or all the same — they would look great on a spotty background or a ticking stripe.

This is quick, easy appliqué of repeated shapes — traditional, yet modern enough to appeal to anyone.

Finished quilt size
Throw, 145 cm (57 inches) square
Finished block size: 16½ inches square including seam allowance

Materials and tools
2 m (80 inches) white quilter's muslin or linen
20 cm (8 inches) each of at least 10 different 1930s prints
40 cm (16 inches) green fabric for leaves
80 cm (32 inches) blue and white striped fabric for sashing
70 cm (28 inches) yellow fabric for border
3.2 m (3½ yards) backing fabric
45 cm (18 inches) red spot fabric for binding
Piece of cotton wadding at least 155 cm (62 inches) square
2B pencil and sharpener
Small piece of template plastic
Small sharp scissors
Appliqué pins
Assorted cotton sewing threads to match leaf and flower fabrics
1 skein green stranded embroidery cotton
2 balls perle cotton No 8 in white for quilting

NOTE: *It is recommended that all fabrics be 100 percent cotton, and be ironed. Requirements are based on fabric 112 cm (44 inches) wide. Unless otherwise stated, all seam allowances are ¼ inch throughout. Colour test any dark fabrics that you are using (see page 177); if they run, wash them before cutting.*

Cutting
All fabrics are strip cut across the width of the fabric, from selvedge to fold (cut off all selvedges first).

FROM THE WHITE FABRIC, CUT:
Nine strips 8½ inches wide. Cross cut these strips into thirty-six squares for the appliqué blocks.
One strip 2½ inches wide. Cross cut this strip into sixteen squares.

Diagram 1 **Appliqué layout**
Note points at which
petals overlap

Leaf and petal template
Seam allowance is not included

FROM THE STRIPED FABRIC, cut twelve strips 2½ inches wide. Cross cut these strips into twenty-four strips 15½ inches long.
FROM THE YELLOW FABRIC, cut eight strips 3 inches wide.
FROM THE BINDING FABRIC, cut seven strips 2½ inches wide.

Appliqué

Draw a seam line ¼ inch inside two corners of a background block using the 2B pencil. Trace the flower shape lightly onto the block, ensuring that the leaf point sits just inside the marked ¼ inch line (see Diagram 1). This is to ensure that your leaf points meet and don't get sewn into the seams.

Trace the leaf/petal shape onto template plastic and cut out carefully with scissors. Choose five fabrics to be the petals for your flower. Using a very sharp 2B pencil, trace one petal onto the front of each fabric, and one onto your leaf fabric. Cut out the petals and the leaf ¼ inch outside the pencil line. (Use a scant ¼ inch, as a large seam allowance is more difficult to turn under.) Using your fingers, press the fabric under along the pencil line all the way around each shape, leaving a sharp crease. Do not iron, as this will leave points in your curves.

Taking care to use the pencil outline of the flower on your block, pin a petal to the background with appliqué pins. Again using the pencil lines you drew as a guide, and thread to match the fabric, slip stitch the petal to the background fabric. Your stitches should just catch the edge of the fabric. Make your stitches as small as possible, and add an extra stitch to secure the points of the petal.

Turn the block over and cut the fabric from the back of each petal using small, sharp scissors (see Diagram 2). Make sure not to cut more than ¼ inch from the seam lines.

Repeat this process with the remaining petals. Remove the background from each petal before applying the next petal. Apply the leaf shapes in the same way. When you have attached all the appliqué shapes, backstitch the stem and vine using two strands of embroidery cotton. One block is now complete. Make a total of 36 appliqué blocks.

Piecing

When you have finished all the appliqué, arrange the blocks into sets of four as shown in the photograph on page 103. Make sure you are happy with the colour placement of each block.

Using a ¼ inch seam allowance, piece the blocks into pairs, taking care that the leaves are all pointing the right direction (that is, into the centre). Press the seams to one side and piece the pairs into a four-patch along the centre seam, taking care to match the seams up at the centre point. Press the seam to one side. You have now completed one four-patch block. Repeat with other appliquéd blocks until you have nine four-patch blocks.

Diagram 2
Cutting away fabric from back of appliqué shapes

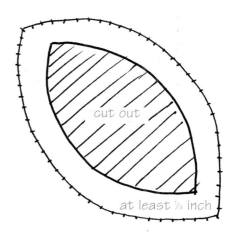

cut out

at least ¼ inch

Place the blocks into rows on the floor or a table so that you cannot make a mistake with your colour placement. Sew the long side of a striped strip to the edge of an appliquéd block. Join the blocks into rows of three, alternating blocks and striped sashing strips, and beginning and ending with a striped strip. You should have three rows of three blocks.

Next, for the sashing rows, join a white 2½ inch square to the end of a blue and white striped strip. Repeat this pattern until you have a row three striped strips long, beginning and ending with a white square. Make four of these.

Pinning from the centre out and taking care to match the seams, pin a striped sashing row to an appliquéd row. Stitch. Repeat, alternating the striped sashing rows and the appliquéd rows, until the centre of the quilt top is sewn together.

Measure the sides of the centre panel and trim the edges if they are not square. Take the yellow fabric strips and sew two together. Press the seams to one side. Measure the strip so that it is the same length as the top of the centre panel and trim to this measurement. Find the centre of the panel and the centre of the border strip and finger-press a crease. Match these points and pin. Next pin the ends, then pin in between, then sew. Press the seam to one side and repeat with the bottom border.

Use the same method to attach the side borders, taking care to measure the size of the quilt with the top and bottom borders attached.

Your quilt top is now complete. Press the entire quilt top carefully.

Backing, quilting and binding

Cut your backing fabric in half into two 1.6 m (64 inch) pieces. Remove the selvedges and stitch together up the middle seam. Press the seam open and press the backing piece carefully.

Refer to pages 192–197 for instructions on finishing.

The flowers and leaves in this quilt were outline quilted using white perle cotton No 8, with cross hatching in the squares and borders.

Girlfriends Galore

Kathy Doughty   ADVANCED

THE IDEA

Hot pink and apple green. The star centre is seen in lots of antique quilts, but in these bright colours it has a modern life of its own.

Choosing fabrics for this quilt is easy, girlfriend! Set the scene with a couple of large florals for the inspirational big borders, then find some stripes, a solid and a few contrasting colours to gossip together. Go shopping with your best friend and it'll happen for you.

Finished quilt size
King single, 174 x 215 cm (68½ x 84¾ inches)

Materials and tools
1.5 m (60 inches) white with pink starburst (or other pattern that can be fussy cut)
70 cm (28 inches) white fabric
2 m (80 inches) light green floral
2 m (80 inches) dark pink and green floral
1 m (40 inches) pink and white stripe fabric; this includes 50 cm (20 inches) for binding
1.85 m (74 inches) hot pink fabric
75 cm (30 inches) light blue floral
4.5 m (5 yds) backing fabric
1.9 x 2.3 m (76 x 92 inch) piece cotton wadding
Neutral-coloured cotton thread for piecing
Rotary cutter, ruler and mat
Kaleidoscope ruler, quarter-square triangle and half-square triangle (optional). Templates are provided for the star diamond triangles, or you can use Kaye England's Nifty Notions ruler set or any 45-degree ruler that makes eight-point stars. It is also recommended that you use a half-square triangle and a quarter-square ruler for accuracy in cutting and piecing this quilt.

NOTE: *It is recommended that all fabrics be 100 percent cotton, and be ironed. Requirements are based on fabric 112 cm (44 inches) wide. Unless otherwise stated, all seam allowances are ¼ inch throughout. Colour test any dark fabrics that you are using (see page 177); if they run, wash them before cutting.*

Cutting
All fabrics are strip cut across the width of the fabric, from selvedge to fold (cut off all selvedges first). Cut the largest pieces first. Please read through the directions before starting.

NOTE: *This quilt can be made using either a standard quilter's ruler or the specialised rulers. The instructions are written first with the strip size for use with the specialised rulers, and then for strips cut using a standard ruler.*

When cutting half-square triangles, if you use the half-square ruler simply cut the strips to the stated width, place the strips face to face and cross cut using the half-square ruler with the blunt end on the top of the strip and the measurement side on the bottom of the strip. Leave the two pieces together and sew as cut, with the diagonal side of the square lined up with a ¼ inch seam. The blunt end of the half-square ruler allows for better accuracy when sewing, as it makes the starting point of the seam obvious.

Using the quarter-square ruler ensures that the bias in the strip is on the inside of the square. Otherwise, this ruler is used in the same manner as the half-square ruler.

Star block

The centre of this block is 26 inches square (finished), with two 2 inch borders adding 4 inches, making the finished block 30 inches square.

FROM THE HOT PINK FABRIC, CUT:

One strip 6 inches wide. Fold in half and cross cut using the Kaleidoscope ruler or the template provided to make 16 diamonds. Some triangles will also be produced from this cutting: save these.

One strip 3 inches wide. Cross cut to give 16 triangles. You will need these plus the remainder from the diamonds to make 32 triangles for the border.

Five strips 4½ inches wide (or 4⅞ inches for those not using the ruler).

FROM THE WHITE FABRIC, CUT:

Two strips 6 inches wide. Fold each strip in half along the length and, using the Kaleidoscope ruler, cut 32 diamonds using the 3 inch line.

Two strips 3 inches wide, then using the ruler cut 60 triangles and eight half triangles.

Two strips 2½ inches wide, then cross cut to give 32 squares.

FROM THE PINK AND WHITE STRIPE FABRIC, CUT:

Two strips 6 inches wide. Fold each strip in half along the length and using the Kaleidoscope ruler, cut 24 diamonds.

Cut one strip 3 inches wide and use the ruler or the template to cut 32 triangles for the border of the star.

Cut eight strips 2½ inches wide for the binding, then sew end to end on the diagonal, matching the stripes carefully.

FROM THE GREEN AND PINK FLORAL, CUT FOR THE SETTING SQUARES AND TRIANGLES:

One strip 8 inches wide, then cross cut this into four 8 inch squares.

One strip 11¾ inches wide, then cross cut one square. Cross cut this

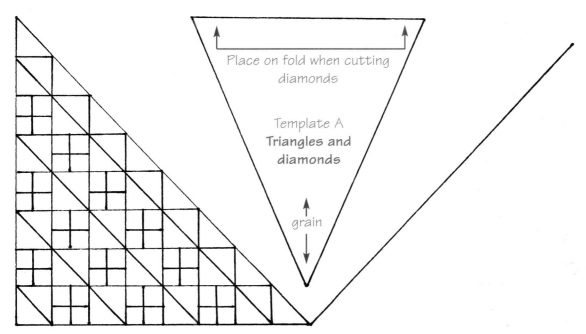

Place on fold when cutting diamonds

Template A
Triangles and diamonds

grain

Diagram 1 **Triangle corners**

Diagram 2 **Rows 8 and 9 (top and bottom of quilt)**

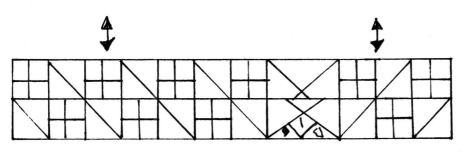

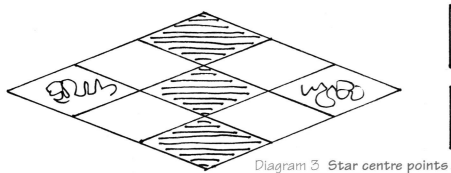

Diagram 3 **Star centre points**

Diagram 4 **Connecting blocks for centre of rows 8 and 9**

Block 1

Block 2

square on both diagonals to give four quarter-square triangles. Use the rest of the fabric to cut 4½ inch strips (or 4⅞ inch strips for those not using the ruler). Set aside.

Three 4½ inch strips (or three 4⅞ inch strips for those not using the ruler). Set aside.

Four 3½ inch squares.

FROM THE LIGHT GREEN FABRIC, CUT:

Two strips 6½ inches wide x 30½ inches long, and two strips 6½ inches wide x 42½ inches long for the inner border.

Eight strips 3½ inches wide for the outer border.

Six strips 2½ inches wide, then cross cut these into 96 squares.

FROM THE PINK STARBURST FABRIC, CUT:

Twenty strips 2½ inches wide, then fussy cut these into 158 squares with the stars approximately in the middle.

Two rectangles 4½ x 7 inches.

FROM THE LIGHT BLUE FLORAL, CUT:

Two strips 2½ inches wide then cross cut these into 48 squares.

Five strips 3¼ inches wide, then using a quarter-square ruler on the 3¼ inch line, cut 64 quarter-square triangles. If you are not using the ruler, cut 16 squares from 5¼ inch wide strips, then cut the squares on both diagonals to give 64 quarter-square triangles.

Two rectangles 4½ x 7 inches.

Sewing

STAR CENTRE ASSEMBLY

Starting with the hot pink outer points, lay out the eight star points as shown in Diagram 3 on page 107. Sew them together in three rows:

1. Hot pink, white, stripe
2. White, stripe, white
3. Stripe, white, hot pink

Sew the rows together carefully, matching the points.

Match the centre points and the points along the seam to join the points of each star point together. Sew four sets together and then four again. Match the centres and sew the two halves together.

The setting squares are then sewn into the corners. Start at the outside point and sew to the star-point joint. Leave the needle down and turn the two pieces so that the seams are aligned, and sew to the next outer point. Press flat. Repeat this process four times.

Next, inset the quarter-square triangles in the same manner.

The star centre will measure 26 inches square.

TRIANGLE BORDER

Starting with a white half triangle, alternate stripe, white and hot pink triangles until the strip has 31 triangles and ends with a white half-triangle on each end. Make four strips in this manner.

Sew a pink starburst square to both ends of two of these strips.

Fold these strips in half and finger-press a crease to mark the centre. Do the same with the star block. Match the centre points and pin, then pin the ends, then pin in between. Sew the borders on to the star centre.

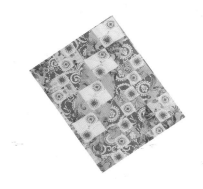

INNER BORDER

Confirm that the centre medallion measures 30½ inches to fit the light green strips. Find the centres of the shorter light green strips and the top and bottom edges of the medallion, match these points, pin and sew.

Attach the two 42½ inch light green strips to the other two sides of the medallion in the same way.

TRIANGLE CORNERS

Refer to Diagram I on page 107. Do not cut the half-square triangles until they are paired up.

With right sides together, match the hot pink 4½ inch fabric strips with the pink and green floral. Cut triangles using the half-square ruler on the 4½ inch line until there are 92 sets. (**NOTE:** If you are not using the ruler, cross cut 4⅞ inch squares and in half diagonally.) Sew along the diagonal to make squares.

Sew the 2½ inch squares of light green to the pink starbursts into pairs, and then into 36 sets of four.

Sew the light blue floral and the pink starbursts into pairs, and then into 24 sets of four.

Sew the white and pink starburst squares into pairs, and then into 16 sets of four.

Match 28 sets of the light blue floral triangles to squares and sew to the pink side as per the diagram. There should be 14 flush left and 14 flush right to form two sets of mirror-image rows.

Lay out each section one at time and work in rows, starting with the light blue quarter square, followed by the pink side of the half-squares.

Next row is the previous set with a light green/pink starburst set.

Next row is the half-square starting with the darker green side.

Next row is the light blue set.

Starting with the longest strips at the outside, pin the strips together, matching all joins, then sew the strips together. Two sets diminish to the right and two sets diminish to the left.

CONNECTING BLOCKS

Start with the light blue rectangle and two 4½ inch squares of the green floral. Line up the corner edges with the square and the rectangle right sides together. Sew diagonally through the centre of the square. Cut ¼ inch away from the seam, open and press flat. Repeat for the other corner. There will be an overlap where the two squares meet (see Diagram 4, Block 1, page 107).

Repeat this process using a rectangle from the starburst fabric, two hot pink squares and two green floral squares (see Diagram 4, Block 2, page 107).

Rows eight and nine for the top and the bottom (see Diagram 2, page 107) are joined in the middle with the connecting blocks and sewn after the triangle corners are attached to the star center.

Borders

Measure the width and the length through the centre of the quilt body. Sew the 3½ inch strips end to end. Trim into four strips: two that measure the width of the quilt and two that measure the length. Sew two green floral squares to the top and bottom strips at both ends of the shorter strips for the top and bottom borders. Find the middle of the border strips and the middle of the body of the quilt and finger-press a crease. Match these points and pin, then pin the ends together, then pin every few inches along the sides. Sew in place and press flat.

Repeat for the top and bottom borders.

Press the entire quilt top carefully.

Backing, quilting and binding

Measure your backing fabric and cut to fit, allowing a little extra, and piecing it if necessary to get the right size.

Refer to pages 192–197 for instructions on finishing.

This quilt was machine quilted using pink cotton and a paisley pattern with an 8 inch repeat.

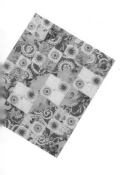

Fanciful Flowers

Sarah Fielke and Kathy Doughty

THE IDEA

This project was inspired by a quilt Kathy saw on a Japanese website, which had pieced blocks and little appliquéd flowers. Sarah designed and stitched the appliqué and Kathy designed and pieced the blocks and did the quilting.

We did this as a range quilt originally. That makes the fabric choices easy, as most ranges have a lot of fabrics that work together. We have since seen it done in moody bohemian colours, pastels and primaries. It's a fun quilt to make, and always gives a good result. Varying the background colour to white, a small spot or a texture gives the quilt a happy lift.

Finished quilt size

King single, 165 x 210 cm (65 x 83 inches)
Finished block size: 18½ inches including seam allowance

Materials and tools

1.4 m (55 inches) brown background fabric
Up to twelve assorted 25 x 50 cm (10 x 20 inch) pieces for appliqué
Fourteen 25 cm (10 inch) pieces of assorted prints for strip piecing, including at least one green for stems
4.5 m (5 yards) backing fabric
50 cm (20 inches) binding fabric
Vliesofix (optional; not needed if you are doing needle-turn appliqué)
Assorted cotton threads to match the appliqué fabrics
Appliqué needles and pins
2B pencil and sharpener
Template plastic
Scissors for fabric
Neutral-coloured cotton thread for piecing
Rotary cutter, mat and ruler
Perle cotton No 8 in pink, yellow, blue and brown for quilting
1.7 x 2.3 m (68 x 91 inch) piece cotton wadding

NOTE: *It is recommended that all fabrics be 100 percent cotton, and be ironed. Requirements are based on fabric 112 cm (44 inches) wide. Unless otherwise stated, all seam allowances are ¼ inch throughout. Colour test any dark fabrics that you are using (see page 177); if they run, wash them before cutting.*
Please read all instructions before starting.

Cutting

All fabrics are strip cut across the width of the fabric (from selvedge to fold). Cut off all selvedges first.

The cutting instructions are labelled alphabetically, but cut the largest pieces first and use the remaining bits to cut the smaller strips.

BLOCK A

FROM THE BROWN BACKGROUND FABRIC, cut six 18½ inch
squares for the appliqué backgrounds.

FROM THE ASSORTED APPLIQUÉ FABRICS, cut the appliqué
shapes as described for Block A, below. Cut the large pieces first. The
leftovers will be used for some of the strips in Block B.

BLOCK B

FROM THE ASSORTED PRINT FABRICS, CUT:

Square A: One strip 6½ inches wide, then cross cut this into six squares
(shown in the photograph as the light blue fabric).

Square B: Eight strips 2½ inches wide, then cross cut these into
126 squares (shown in the photograph as the orange fabric).

Square B1: One 2½ inch square from each of two different colours for the
bottom border.

FROM THE REMAINING FABRICS, including the leftover appliqué
fabrics, cut a total of fifty strips 2½ inches wide.

FROM THE BINDING FABRIC, cut eight strips 2½ inches wide.

Appliqué for Block A

Instructions are given here for needle-turn appliqué, but you could just as
easily use Vliesofix and blanket stitch the shapes down.

First, make your stems. Using the 45-degree angle on your patchwork
ruler, cut bias strips ¾ inch wide from the green fabric. The pieces don't
have to be too long, as each stem is only short. Fold under ¼ inch on each
side of the strip and press to make a strip ¼ inch wide. You will need six
strips at least 6 inches long. Refer to Diagram 3 on page 118.

Trace each appliqué shape onto template plastic and cut out using
paper scissors. Decide which colours to use for the various parts of the
first flower.

Fold the background square into halves, then quarters, and finger press
the creases to find the centre of the block.

Using a sharp 2B pencil, trace one seed pod, two pollen, two petals
and ten seeds onto the front of the appropriate fabrics. Take care to leave
space between the pieces for seam allowance. Using sharp fabric scissors,
cut the shapes out of the fabric a scant ¼ inch outside of the pencil line.

Using your fingers, press the edges of the fabric along the pencil line,
making a sharp, smooth crease. Do not iron, as this will make points in the
curves. Position the pieces on the background block using the photograph
as a guide. Using short pins, pin the pieces to the background. Take into
account that the stem will go underneath the main seed pod of the flower,
as will the petals and the pollen pieces. The dotted lines on the template
pieces indicate which parts of each piece should be placed under the

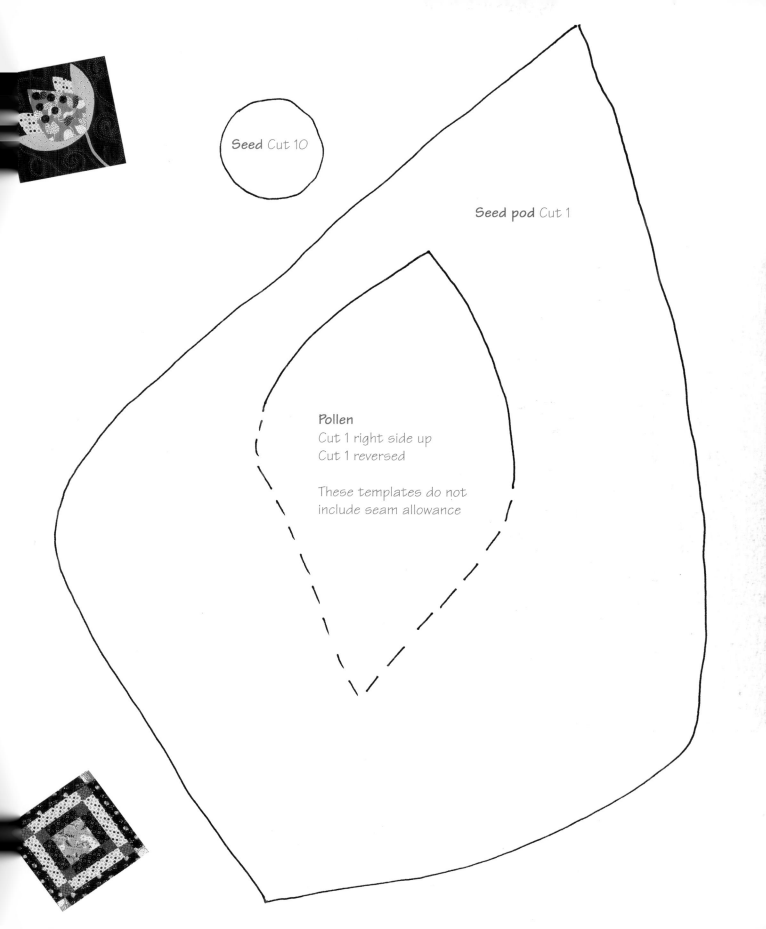

Seed Cut 10

Seed pod Cut 1

Pollen
Cut 1 right side up
Cut 1 reversed

These templates do not
include seam allowance

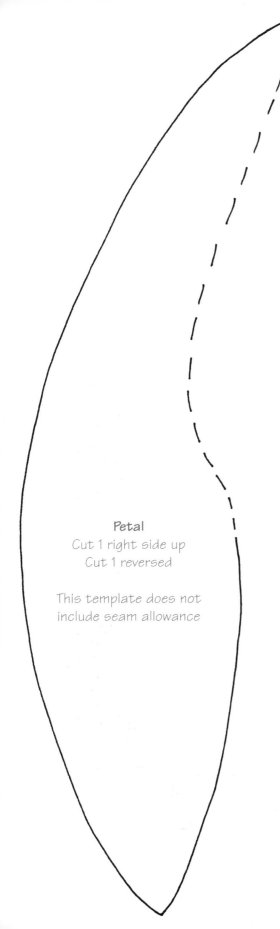

Petal
Cut 1 right side up
Cut 1 reversed

This template does not
include seam allowance

adjacent pieces. Using thread to match the piece you are appliquéing, slip-stitch the piece to the background fabric. Your stitches should just catch the edge of the fabric. Make your stitches as small as possible, and add an extra stitch to secure any points.

Turn the block over and make a small cut at the back of the shape, taking care not to cut the applique. Cut the background away underneath the flower. Be sure not to cut closer than $\frac{1}{4}$ inch away from the seam lines.

Repeat this process with the next shape. Remove the background from under each piece before applying the next one.

Repeat this process until you have six blocks.

Sewing

BLOCK B ASSEMBLY

Refer to Diagram 2 on page 118.

Set your strips into six piles of one A, twelve B, four D, four F, and four G strips. Be sure to choose your fabrics to alternate the strips so that they contrast as you move away from the centre square.

Sew a D strip to both sides of the centre block A.

Sew a B square to both ends of two D strips.

Pin the seams and sew the strips to the centre block so that the B squares are in all four corners stepping out from the square.

Continue in this manner until the block has three strips on all sides. The finished block should measure $18\frac{1}{2}$ inches square.

Make six B blocks in total.

When you have completed six appliqué blocks and six pieced blocks, arrange them in four alternating rows of three. Be sure to angle the flower stems in different directions to add interest. The flower blocks must be placed in the middle of the top and third rows; this is important for the border to work correctly. Check for colour balance as you go.

Match and pin all seams, then sew the blocks together in rows.

Match and pin all seams, then sew the rows together into columns.

Borders

Refer to Diagram 1 opposite. At this point it is a good idea to set out the remaining strips for placement in order to continue to alternate light and dark colours through the borders.

Strip sizes for the borders are as follows:

B — $2\frac{1}{2}$ x $2\frac{1}{2}$ inches
C — $2\frac{1}{2}$ x $4\frac{1}{2}$ inches
D — $2\frac{1}{2}$ x $6\frac{1}{2}$ inches
E — $2\frac{1}{2}$ x $8\frac{1}{2}$ inches
F — $2\frac{1}{2}$ x $10\frac{1}{2}$ inches
G — $2\frac{1}{2}$ x $14\frac{1}{2}$ inches

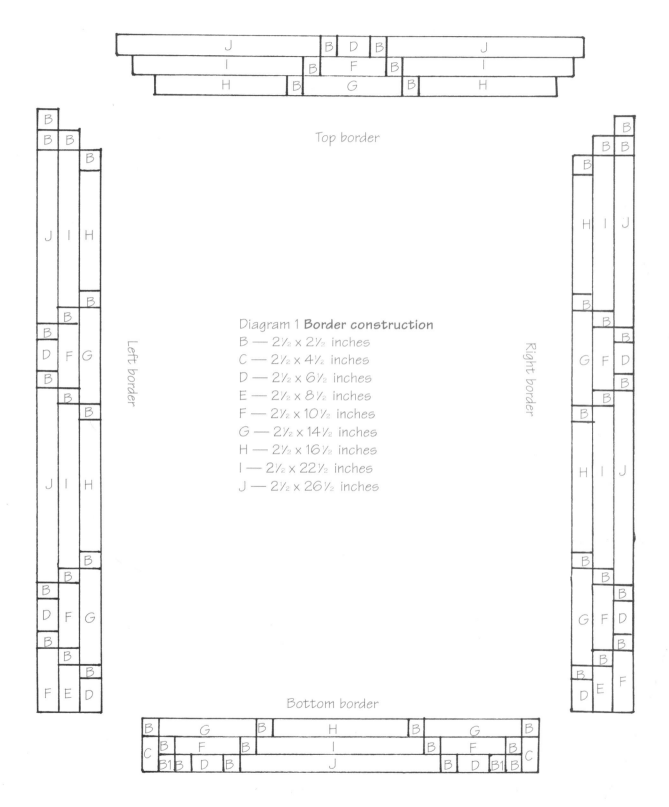

Top border

Left border

Right border

Diagram 1 **Border construction**

B — 2½ x 2½ inches
C — 2½ x 4½ inches
D — 2½ x 6½ inches
E — 2½ x 8½ inches
F — 2½ x 10½ inches
G — 2½ x 14½ inches
H — 2½ x 16½ inches
I — 2½ x 22½ inches
J — 2½ x 26½ inches

Bottom border

Diagram 2 **Block B**
(18½ inches square)
A — 6½ x 6½ inches
B — 2½ x 2½ inches
D — 2½ x 6½ inches
F — 2½ x 10½ inches
G — 2½ x 14½ inches
Make 6

Diagram 3 **Block A**
(18½ inches square)
Use templates on pages 115–116
Make 6

I — 2½ x 22½ inches
J — 2½ x 26½ inches

The bottom three-row border can be fully assembled. Pin all the pieces together as per the diagram, one strip at a time, then sew together. Pin then sew the three rows together to complete the border, then sew it to the bottom edge of the quilt, matching the seams of all B squares as you go.

The remaining borders are pieced, pinned and sewn to the quilt, one row at a time, as follows:

1. Inside row of the top border to the top of the quilt, ending with the H strips.
2. Inside right side, then the inside left side strips.
3. Middle row of the top border.
4. Middle row on the right side, then the left.
5. Outer row of the top border.
6. Outer row on the right side and then the left.

The quilt top is now complete. Press the entire top carefully.

Backing, quilting and binding

Measure your backing fabric and cut to fit, allowing a little extra, and piecing it if necessary to get the right size.

Refer to pages 192–197 for instructions on finishing.

This quilt was quilted in perle cotton No 8 to match the background fabric. Draw a free-flowing swirling line around the appliqué with chalk or a 2B pencil. Quilt the line with the background perle cotton and then work around the line with alternating colours. In the pieced blocks, use masking tape or a 2B pencil line to cross hatch diagonally through the squares.

Dotty for Dresden

Sarah Fielke

ADVANCED

THE IDEA

I love to look at antique quilts, and it often surprises me how 'modern' they are. We perceive antique quilts to be traditional and dull coloured, but the more I look the more I find that would be wild even by today's standards. This quilt was inspired by an antique quilt in a book, which incorporated Dresden plates with red circles between them. I loved the repetition of the appliquéd circles, the circles of the plates and the circles created in the space between the plates. Why not take circles to the max and add spots? When it comes to my quilts, too many spots are never enough! The spots are the secret here; they need to be the reverse of each other to achieve balance. You could easily switch colours, though — try blue, green or a solid background colour.

Quilt size

Double bed, 174 x 248 cm (68½ x 97½ inches)
Finished block size: 15½ inches including seam allowance

Materials and tools

6 m (6½ yards) red on cream spot for background

1.6 m (66 inches) cream on red spot for appliqué circles and binding

30 cm (12 inches) each of at least sixteen different fabrics, totalling 4.8 m (5⅓ inches); or use scraps

Nifty Notions 22.5 degree Wedge ruler (this is optional, but the ruler does all the mathematics for you; sixteen 22.5-degree wedges = 360 degrees, which is a circle)

Sheet of template plastic (optional)

50 cm (20 inches) freezer paper

2B pencil and sharpener

Hand appliqué needles

Rotary cutter, ruler and mat

Cream and red cotton threads for appliqué and piecing

Small sharp scissors for snipping

Scissors for template plastic

Fabric scissors

Perle cotton No 8 in cream for quilting

195 x 270 cm (78 x 108 inches) piece cotton wadding

5.4 m (6 yards) backing fabric

NOTE: *It is recommended that all fabrics be 100 percent cotton, and be ironed. Requirements are based on fabric 112 cm (44 inches) wide. Unless otherwise stated, all seam allowances are ¼ inch throughout. Colour test any dark fabrics that you are using (see page 177); if they run, wash them before cutting.*

Instructions are given here to make this quilt using either a Nifty Notions ruler, or templates. We recommend the ruler as a quick, easy and accurate method of making Dresden Plates.

Please read all instructions before starting.

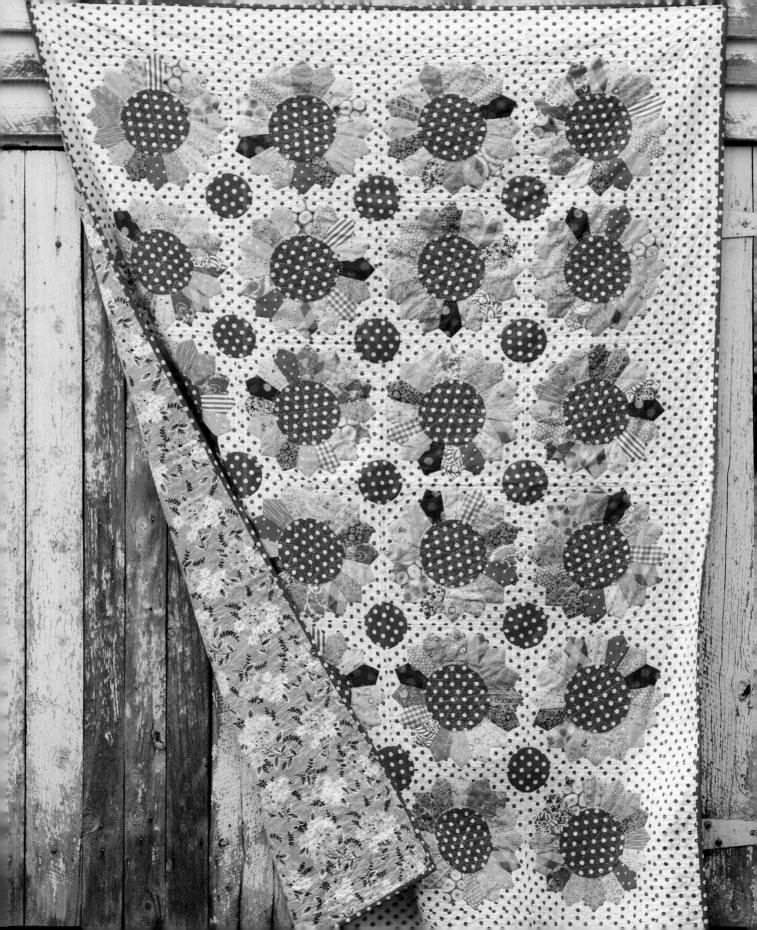

Preparation

FROM THE TEMPLATE PLASTIC, trace with the 2B pencil and cut accurately on the drawn line:

One Template A piece (page 124). This does not include seam allowance.

One Template B piece (page 124). This does not include seam allowance.

One Template C piece (opposite). This includes a ¼ inch seam allowance. If you are using a wedge ruler, refer to Diagram 1 and omit cutting Template C. Label all templates and transfer all markings.

Cutting

FROM THE RED SPOT ON CREAM FABRIC, CUT:

Twelve strips 15½ inches wide. Cross cut these strips to yield twenty-four squares for the background. You will get two squares from each strip.

Ten strips 5½ inches wide. Cross cut these strips to yield twenty strips 5½ x 15½ inches and four 5½ inch squares for the border.

FROM THE CREAM SPOT ON RED FABRIC:

Trace fifteen Template A circles onto the back of the fabric then cut out using fabric scissors, allowing a scant ¼ inch seam allowance.

Trace twenty-four Template B circles onto the back of the fabric then cut out using fabric scissors, allowing a scant ¼ inch seam allowance.

Cut nine strips 3 inches wide for the binding.

FROM THE FREEZER PAPER, trace around circle templates A and B along the dotted line onto the paper side and cut out with paper scissors on the drawn line. These templates do not include the seam allowance. You should only need about twelve or fifteen of each circle, as the freezer paper will be peeled off and reused.

FROM THE SIXTEEN ASSORTED FABRICS:

If you are not using the wedge ruler, trace and cut 384 of Template C for the Dresden Plate blocks.

If you are using the wedge ruler, for a plate as pictured, cut two strips 4½ inches wide from each of your sixteen fabrics.

For the 22.5 degree wedges, place the wedge ruler on the strip so that the 2-inch mark lines up with the bottom of the strip. Refer to Diagram 1 for details. (To make plates to fit the background squares for this project, all the wedges are cut with the bottom of the strip on the 2 inch mark of the ruler. To make larger or smaller plates, you can move the ruler up or down the strip, to the 1-inch or even the 3-inch mark. This will result in different sized plates with larger or smaller holes in the centre.) Using your rotary cutter, cut a piece the same shape as the ruler from the strip. Turn the ruler upside down so that the wedge faces the other direction, and line the 2 inch mark up with the top of the strip. Cut another piece. Repeat until you have twelve pieces from each strip, for a total of 384 blades, sixteen for each of twenty-four blocks.

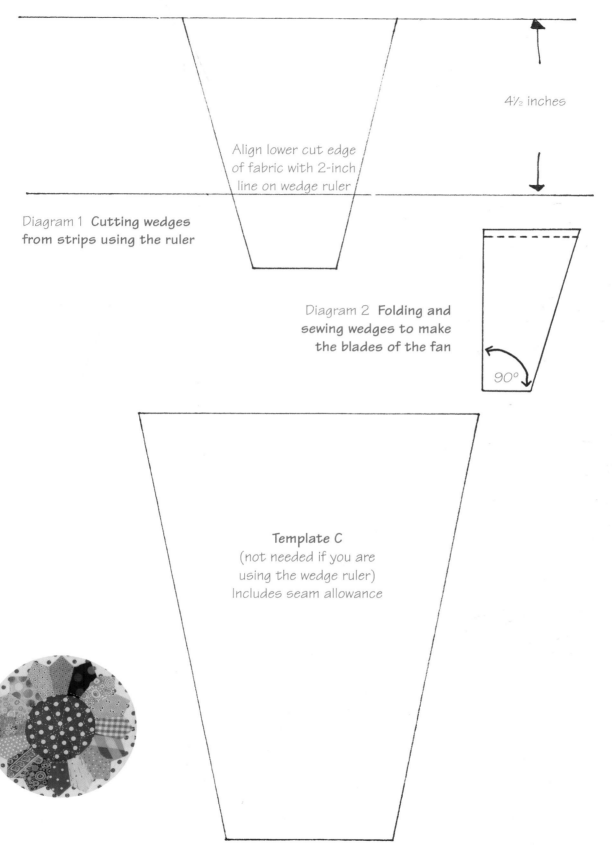

4½ inches

Align lower cut edge
of fabric with 2-inch
line on wedge ruler

Diagram 1 **Cutting wedges
from strips using the ruler**

Diagram 2 **Folding and
sewing wedges to make
the blades of the fan**

90°

Template C
(not needed if you are
using the wedge ruler)
Includes seam allowance

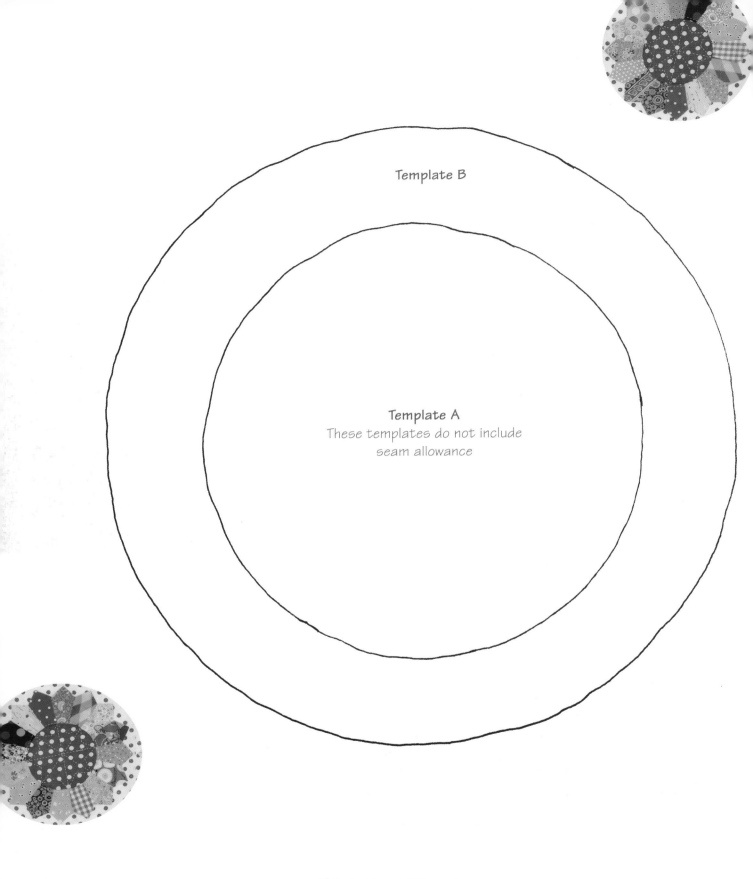

Template B

Template A
These templates do not include
seam allowance

Sewing

For the Dresden Plates, fold each of the wedges in half lengthwise with right sides together, and sew along the top edge (see Diagram 2, page 123). This is an excellent time to chain piece, as there are a lot of wedges!

Turn the wedges right side out, taking care to poke the point out so it is nice and sharp, and then press the wedges flat, with the seam at the back aligning with the centre line of the wedge.

Sew the wedges together along the long raw edges, one after another, and alternating them to form a colour pattern, e.g. pink, green, blue, orange, pink, green etc. Repeat until you have sewn 16 wedges together, then sew the first and last wedges together to complete a circle. Press. You have now completed one plate.

Repeat these steps until you have made 24 plates.

Appliquéing the Dresden Plates

When you have made 24 plates, you can begin to appliqué them down. Fold a background square in half, then in quarters and finger-press to mark the centre of each edge. Position a Dresden Plate piece onto the background square so it is centred, using the points of the blades as a guide, and pin in place. If you find that your plate is too large for the square, you may need to adjust your seams to a more generous ¼ inch.

Pin or baste the plate to the square, around both the outer and the inner edges. Using cream thread, hand appliqué the plate to the background square around the outside edge.

Next, iron a freezer-paper circle, plastic side down, to the back of each Template B circle and finger-press the fabric over the edges. Position a red spot circle over the hole in the centre of the plate, centre and pin in place. Hand appliqué the circle to the block using red thread. Turn the block over and cut the fabric away behind the circle, ¼ inch out from the seam, taking care not to cut the red fabric. Remove the freezer paper for reuse. Repeat this process until you have appliquéd all the plates down.

Construction

Lay your blocks out on the floor or on a design wall in six rows of four and arrange them until you are happy with their placement.

Beginning with the top row, take a 5½ x 15 inch border strip and sew it to the first block using a ¼ inch seam. Next, attach a Plate block. Repeat until you have a row of four blocks that begins and ends with a border strip. Make six strips in this manner.

Take the remaining border pieces and sew two rows of four by four strips lengthwise, beginning and ending with a 5½ inch square. Taking care to match the seams, pin then sew these two strips to the top and bottom of the quilt. Press.

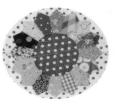

Appliquéing the small circles

Take the remaining red circles and iron a Template A freezer-paper circle, plastic side down, to the back. Fold into quarters and finger-press. Applique the circle into the space created between the plates, matching the seams to the folds in the circles to centre them. Refer to the photograph opposite for details. Repeat with the remaining circles.

The quilt top is now complete. Press the entire quilt top well.

Backing, quilting and binding

Measure your backing fabric and cut it to fit, allowing a little extra, and piecing it if necessary to get the right size.

Refer to pages 192–197 for instructions on finishing.

Dotty for Dresden was quilted using cream perle cotton No 8. The background was quilted in a checkerboard pattern 1 inch apart, and a star design was quilted into the centre of all the red spotted circles.

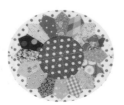

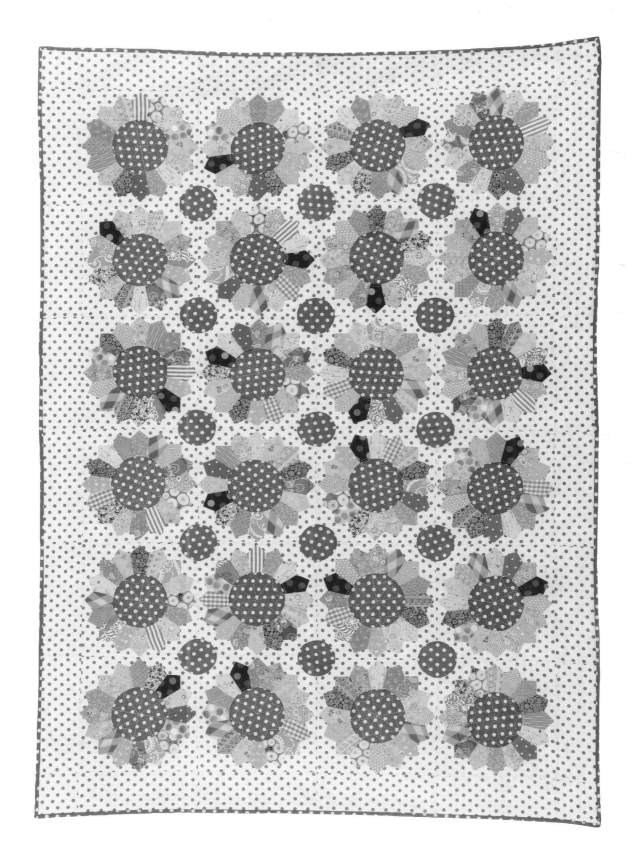

Three-ring Circus

Kathy Doughty

ADVANCED

THE IDEA

The retro circus-print fabric brought to mind circus tents in spots and stripes. A few quick cuts with a 60-degree ruler, and the tents were whirling around the tall man and his friends.

Of course circus prints are perfect for this quilt, but any retro-styled kids' print works. We have used dogs, cats, flowers and even elephants to make these circus-tent tops come to life. The alternating spots and stripes are lively, adding motion to the hexagons and perfectly complementing the primary colours in the circus fabric. Use your imagination and have fun.

Finished quilt size

Cot size, 110 x 125 cm (43¼ x 49¼ inches)
Finished block size: 16½ inches from flat side to flat side including seam allowance

Materials and tools

100 cm (40 inches) circus feature print for large hexagons
15 cm (6 inches) clown print for small hexagons
25 cm (10 inch) strips of 8 combinations of spots and stripes for circus tents
50 cm (20 inches) binding fabric
145 cm (58 inches) backing fabric
140 x 150 cm (55 x 60 inch) piece polyester wadding
Neutral-coloured cotton thread
Creative Grids 8-inch 60-degree ruler
Purchased hexagon template, size 5 inches, or use the template provided
Paper for templates
Quarter-inch ruler
2B pencil and sharpener
Masking tape, 2.5 cm (1 inch) wide
Perle cotton No 8 in cream for quilting

Cutting

Cut 8½ inch strips of all stripe and spot fabrics and remove the selvedges.
For stripe half-triangles: Starting at the left-hand side of the stripe fabric strip and using the centre line of the ruler, cut six left-hand triangles of each colour. See Diagram 1 on page 131.
For spot half-triangles: Starting at the left-hand side of the spot fabric strip and using the centre line of the ruler, cut six right-hand half-triangles of each colour. See Diagram 2 on page 131.

NOTE: *To put the triangles together so that the pattern rotates, it is important to confirm that the stripe will be on the left hand side of the triangle. If you are confident with the ruler, cut the strips with a spot and stripe fabric together, right sides facing.*

Sewing spot/strip hexagons

Pin then sew the centre seam of the triangles together in spot/stripe pairs, and then in sets to form six full hexagons and four half hexagons. Match and pin the centres and ends before sewing the halves together.

Hexagon appliqué

Use the 5-inch hexagon template to make eight paper templates. Outline the hexagon on the back of the feature fabric, then mark a ¼ inch seam allowance as well. Cut out the hexagons and then baste them to the paper templates, turning over the seam allowance smoothly around the edge.

Match up the corners of the 5-inch hexagons in the feature fabric to the seams in the triangle hexagons and stitch in place. When this is complete, make a cut into the back, carefully trim away from behind and remove the paper template. Complete six in this manner and set aside.

Cut the last two hexagons in half through the centre of the flat side, allowing for a ¼ inch seam. Cut two of the 5-inch hexagons in half through the points, allowing for a ¼ inch seam, before sewing to the larger half-hexagons for the borders.

Trace your finished pieced hexagon onto a large piece of paper to form a template for the feature fabric. It should measure 14¾ by 16¾ inches (measuring from flat side to flat side and point to point respectively). Cut five full hexagons. Cut two of these hexagons in half from the top centre to the bottom and one in half from the side centre to the other side. Be careful to watch the direction of the feature print as two will be on the top and bottom while the other two halves are on the sides.

Sewing

To inset-piece the hexagons together, start by first matching from point to point on one side. Pin and sew carefully to the next point exactly. Leave the needle down, lift the foot and turn the fabric so that you are now facing the next point. Start sewing to the next point and repeat. Press to the dark side as you go and check your points for accuracy. Inset piece all of the hexagons together to form the top.

Backing, quilting and binding

Measure your backing fabric and cut it to fit, allowing a little extra, and piecing it if necessary to get the right size.

Refer to pages 192–197 for instructions on finishing.

Cream perle cotton No 8 was used to quilt concentric lines in the spot and stripe hexagons, using masking tape to mark out the quilting lines, and to quilt around the animals on the circus fabric.

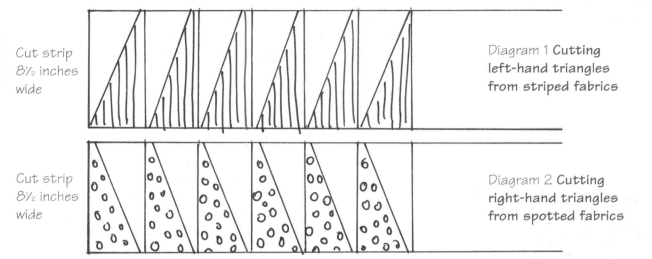

Cut strip
8½ inches
wide

Diagram 1 **Cutting
left-hand triangles
from striped fabrics**

Cut strip
8½ inches
wide

Diagram 2 **Cutting
right-hand triangles
from spotted fabrics**

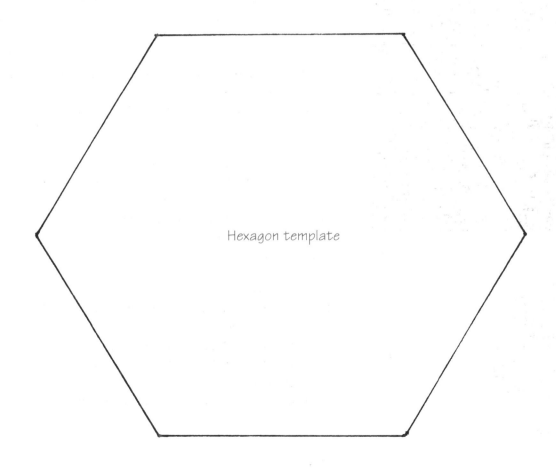

Hexagon template

The Big Pineapple

Sarah Fielke

THE IDEA

The Big Pineapple was inspired totally by the fabric and my need to make a pineapple-block quilt, which happened to coincide. However, with the fabric print being so big and pineapple blocks traditionally being so small, I did the only logical thing and enlarged the block to fit the flower.

The key to selecting colours for this quilt is in your inspiration fabric centre square. Once you choose that, you can pull all your colour choices from there. I would love to see this quilt done in civil war fabrics for a change of pace.

Finished quilt size

King, 250 cm (98 inches) square
Finished block size: 26½ inches square including seam allowance

Materials and tools

60 cm (24 inches) centre floral (if you want to fussy cut the flowers, you need four whole and eight half flowers, and the half flowers need to have the straight grain of the fabric on the long side of the triangle)
20 cm (8 inches) each of at least eight different pinks and oranges
1.3 m (52 inches) turquoise, for the constant triangles in each block
25 cm (10 inches) each of at least eight different greens or turquoises
1.1 m (43 inches) plain green for sashing
2 m (80 inches) pink spot for border
65 cm (26 inches) binding fabric
6.8 m (7½ yds) backing fabric (or 5.4 m/6 yds plus a strip of joined scraps from the front equalling 50 cm/20 inches wide)
Rotary cutter, ruler and mat
Cotton thread for piecing
2.7 m (3 yd) square of wadding
Perle cotton No 8 in aqua for quilting
1-inch wide masking tape for quilting

NOTE: *It is recommended that all fabrics be 100 percent cotton, and be ironed. Requirements are based on fabric 112 cm (44 inches) wide. Unless otherwise stated, all seam allowances are ¼ inch throughout. Colour test any dark fabrics that you are using (see page 177); if they run, wash them before cutting.*

Before you begin

This quilt is a bit confusing to start with, so please read here first.

The Big Pineapple has four 'pineapple' blocks set on point, surrounded by eight half blocks, two on each side of the quilt. All letters throughout the pattern refer to labels on the block diagram (see Diagram 3 on page 136).

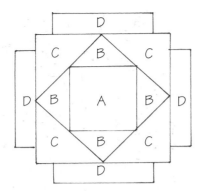

Diagram 1

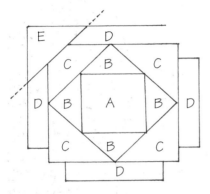

Diagram 2

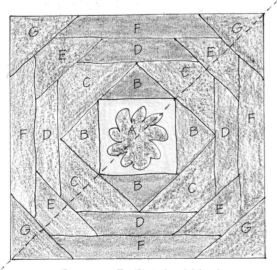

Diagram 3 **Finished block**
(The dotted line indicates the
construction of the half-blocks.)

The centre of each block is a large pink flower print fussy cut to feature the flower. As the pieces are joined to each centre block, there are two colour groups used: at right angles to the centre, pink and orange fabrics are used (in pieces B, D and F — see Diagram 3). The diagonal pieces (C, G and E) are turquoise and green. In each block too, the opposite pieces are made of the same fabric; that is, the pieces B, D and F going 'north' and 'south' are all cut from one pink or orange fabric, and the B, D and F pieces going 'east' and 'west' are all cut from a different pink or orange fabric. The same fabric is used in each of the two diagonal directions also.

Cutting

FROM THE CENTRE FLORAL FABRIC, CUT:
One strip 9 inches wide. From this, cross cut or fussy cut four 9 inch
 centre squares (shape A).
From the remaining fabric, cut two 13¼ squares, then cut each square in
 quarters diagonally to form eight centre triangles (half shapes A).

FROM EACH OF THE THE PINK AND ORANGE FABRICS, CUT:
One strip 7 inches wide. From each of these strips cut two 7-inch squares.
 Cross cut these squares along one diagonal to make two half-square
 triangles (shape B). You should have 32 triangles.
From the remainder of each of the fabrics, cut two strips 32 inches long x
 2¾ inches wide, or two strips to co-ordinate with each of the B squares.
 You should have 32 strips in total (for shapes D and F).

FROM THE TURQUOISE FABRIC, CUT FOR THE WHOLE BLOCKS:
Four 9½ inch squares, then cut these in half along one diagonal to form
 eight triangles (shape C).
Four 7¾ inch squares, then cut these in half along one diagonal to form
 eight triangles (shape E).
Four 7 inch squares, then cut these in half along one diagonal to form
 eight triangles (shape G).

FROM THE TURQUOISE FABRIC, CUT FOR THE HALF BLOCKS:
Four 7 inch squares, then cut these in half along one diagonal to form
 eight triangles (half shape C).
Four 6 inch squares, then cut these in half along one diagonal to form
 eight triangles (half shape E).
Four 5½ inch squares, then cut these in half along one diagonal to form
 eight triangles (half shape G).

**FROM THE VARIOUS GREEN OR TURQUOISE FABRICS, CUT
 A TOTAL OF:**
Four 9½ inch squares, then cut these in half along one diagonal to form
 eight triangles (shape C).
Four 7¾ inch squares, then cut these in half along one diagonal to form
 eight triangles (shape E).

Four 7 inch squares, then cut these in half along one diagonal to form eight triangles (shape G).

NOTE: *Take care to cut one set of each shape per block.*

FROM THE SASHING FABRIC, cut twenty-two strips 2 inches wide.

FROM THE PINK BORDER FABRIC, cut nine strips 8½ inches wide.

FROM THE BINDING FABRIC, cut ten strips 2½ inches wide. Join these on the bias.

Sewing

WHOLE PINEAPPLE BLOCKS

Sew four pink or orange B triangles, one to each side of the A square. Sew two turquoise C triangles to two opposite sides of the AB square. Sew two green or turquoise C triangles to the other two opposite sides of the AB square.

Starting and finishing 1½ inches from each corner, sew a strip D (14 inches long) of the same fabric as the nearest B triangle. Repeat on the opposite side, then again with fabric to match the other two sides. Refer to Diagram 1 opposite.

Matching fabric to the adjacent C triangle, pin then sew an E triangle so that its outside edges line up with the edges of the adjacent D strips. Refer to Diagram 2 opposite.

Repeat with the same E triangle in the opposite corner, then the two E triangles that match the other diagonal.

In the same way as for the D strip above, attach an F strip that matches the D strip it touches, starting and finishing 1½ inches from the corners. The strip will be 18½ inches long.

Repeat the previous step on the opposite side of the block, then repeat for the other two sides with matching fabric.

In the same way as for the E triangle above, align, pin and sew the respective G triangles, matching the fabric again.

You have now completed one whole block. Make three more whole Pineapple blocks.

HALF PINEAPPLE BLOCKS

Following the instructions above, but with the half triangles C, E and G from the turquoise fabric, make eight half pineapple blocks.

SASHING

Using the 22 green sashing strips, join four pairs together into long strips for the outside edge of the quilt centre. Join three strips together for the long diagonal and join two lots of two for the two short diagonal strips. You should have four strips remaining.

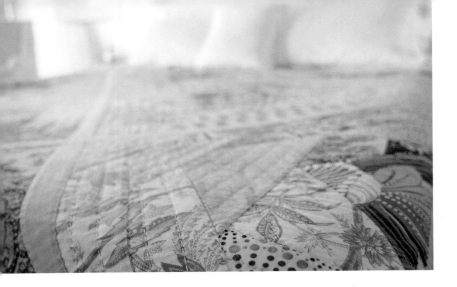

Arrange the four large pineapple blocks on point, with the turquoise fabric meeting at the centre. Arrange the eight half blocks, two on each side, with the turquoise fabric along the outside edges.

Put the eight short sashing strips between the blocks in one direction. There will be four rows to join up — triangle, sashing, triangle (twice), and triangle, sashing, square, sashing, square, sashing, triangle (twice).

Join the four rows together with the relevant longer sashes between the rows.

Measure the size of the pieced panel through the middle. Trim the long outer sashing strips to this measurement. Find the centre of the outside sashing strip and the centre of the edge of the pieced blocks and finger-press a crease. Match these points and pin. Pin the ends, pin in between, then sew. Repeat with the opposite border, and then with either side.

Borders

Join the pink border strips in two lots of two strips, and two lots of two and a half strips. Measure the quilt top through the centre and trim the top and bottom strips to fit this length. Find the centre of the edge of the quilt and the centre of one strip and finger-press a crease. Match these points and pin together. Pin the ends, pin in between, then sew. Repeat with the bottom border, then attach the side borders using the same method.

Press the entire quilt top carefully.

Backing, quilting and binding

Measure your backing fabric and cut to fit, allowing a little extra, and piecing it if necessary to get the right size.

See pages 192–197 for instructions on finishing. The Big Pineapple was quilted using perle cotton No 8 in straight lines 1 inch apart over the whole quilt. You can use 1-inch masking tape to achieve a similar linear result.

Ginger Snap

Kathy Doughty   ADVANCED

THE IDEA

Ginger Snap was inspired by the fabric, which I fell in love with instantly. Fabric ranges today are perfectly structured for this quilt. First, find one large-patterned fabric with a number of colours to establish your palette. Then choose four to five medium-scale patterns with colours that relate to those in the main fabric. When piecing the strips, work through the value scale in your colour palette from light to dark.

This is a great opportunity to use up some of the fabrics in your stash. Try spots, solids, stripes, pretty florals, whatever. If something is very strong in colour or value, use less of it, but use it anyway.

Finished quilt size

Queen, 204 x 190 cm (80 x 75 inches)

Materials and tools

2.6 m (102 inches) main 'inspiration' fabric

30 cm (12 inches) of each of 4–5 secondary fabrics for the solid triangles

3 m (120 inches) in total of an assortment of strip scraps for the strip-pieced triangles

110 cm (44 inches) inner border fabric

90 cm (36 inches) binding fabric

4.4 m (5 yds) backing fabric

Rotary cutter, ruler and mat

60-degree triangle ruler

Neutral-coloured cotton thread for piecing

2.2 x 2.4 m (88 x 96 inch) piece cotton wadding

4–6 balls perle cotton No 8 for hand-quilting

NOTE: *It is recommended that all fabrics be 100 percent cotton, and be ironed. Requirements are based on fabric 112 cm (44 inches) wide. Unless otherwise stated, all seam allowances are ¼ inch throughout. Colour test any dark fabrics that you are using (see page 177); if they run, wash them before cutting.*

Please read all instructions before starting. See pages 186–187 for instructions on using the 60-degree angle ruler.

Cutting

FROM THE INSPIRATION FABRIC, cut 3 strips 8½ inches wide.

Establish a straight edge at the right end. Unfold to a single layer. Place the pointed end of the ruler at the bottom of the right-hand end of the strip and the base of the ruler at the top, with the dotted line to the right of centre on the straight end. Place a second ruler against the 60-degree ruler and cut along the diagonal edge of the second ruler after removing the 60-degree ruler. The cut-away piece is a half-triangle.

Diagram 1 **Quilt construction**

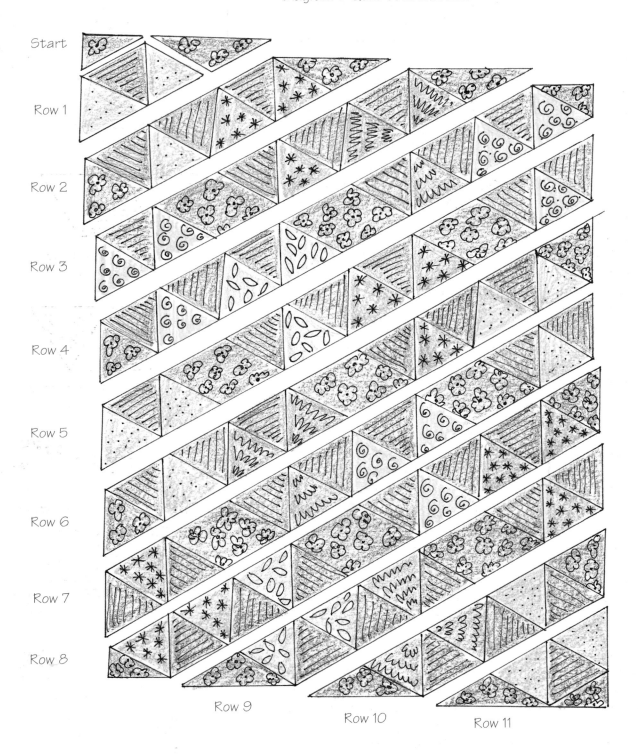

Start

Row 1

Row 2

Row 3

Row 4

Row 5

Row 6

Row 7

Row 8

Row 9

Row 10

Row 11

Measure 10⅛ inches from the right bottom to the left, mark with a pencil and do the same for the top. Use the 60-degree ruler (or the 60-degree line on your straight ruler) and cut a diagonal line between the points. Repeat twice to create three diamonds. When these are cut, fold them in half with a fold at the widest point. Use the ruler to trim to the exact shape, with the 8¼ inch line resting on the fold of the diamond. The remaining fabric in this strip will yield a triangle. Repeat until you have nine diamonds, three triangles and three half-triangles.

Cut two more strips 8½ inches wide. Establish a straight edge at both ends. Line up the left end with the dotted line to the left of the centre line on the ruler and cut along the diagonal to reveal a half-triangle. Use the full size of the ruler and cut seven triangles, ending with a half-triangle. Repeat for the second strip. You should now have fourteen triangles (one is extra), ten half-triangles and the nine diamonds.

Cut three strips 5¼ inches wide. Establish a straight edge on both ends of the strip. Use a previously cut half-triangle as a guide and cut along the diagonal from the right end of the strip. Cut away the half-triangle and fold the pointed end until the ruler fits to cut a half-diamond. The dotted line to the left of the centre will line up with the bottom of the strip, and the 8¼ inch line will line up with the folded end. Cut along the diagonal and repeat until there are four half-diamonds. End with a half-triangle.

FROM THE COMPLIMENTARY FABRICS, cut 63 triangles.

FROM THE BORDER FABRIC, cut seven strips 5½ inches wide.

Creating pieced strips for triangles

Select fabrics from your stash for the strip triangles. Cut them into strips of varying widths, from 1–3 inches. Sew along the length and press the seams to the left. Make the sets of strips 17 inches in height and at least 10½ inches long. Use the ruler in the same manner as above to make 61 triangles, one half-triangle and eight half-diamonds from the strips.

Lastly, cut four 5½ inch squares from the pieced strips.

The best way to avoid warping is to cut the strips in equal lengths and match them while sewing.

TIP: Use a variety of scraps and don't be afraid to make brave choices that push the colour, texture or depth of the recipe for the quilt.

Sewing

Select 16 sets of six triangles, each with three solid triangles and three strip triangles. Pin then sew a solid, a strip and a solid together along the long sides to form a half-hexagon. See Diagram 3. Do the same with the rest of the triangles, this time sewing together a strip triangle, a solid and a strip from each set. See Diagram 4. Put the half-hexagons aside.

Diagram 2
Shapes made using a 60-degree ruler

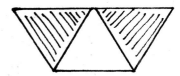

Diagram 3 Half hexagon 1
(solid/strip/solid)

Diagram 4 Half hexagon 2
(strip/solid/strip)

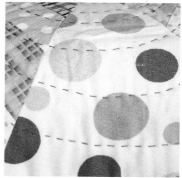

The quilt is assembled in diagonal rows that join the half-hexagons into whole hexagons: see Diagram I on page 142. When all of your triangles are combined into half-hexagons, lay them out on a large flat space in rows to match up the pairs. This is best done on a design wall or a sheet taped to the wall so you can check for colour balance at the same time.

Starting in the top left-hand corner, first pin, then sew the half-triangle to the long edge of the middle triangle of the half-hexagon in the next row. Take a half-diamond border piece in the main fabric and pin then sew it to the right-hand triangle of the same half-hexagon. These pieces together form a wedge shape. This is the first diagonal row.

Pin the diagonal rows, one at a time, and sew together, being sure to pin and match the centre points of the hexagons for accuracy. Continue in this manner until all the rows are complete and sewn together.

Borders

Measure the quilt through the middle to determine both the length and width. Piece the 5½ inch strips together to fit these lengths.

First, attach the top and bottom inner borders.

To both ends of each long inner border piece, sew a strip-pieced square. Sew these inner borders to the quilt body, matching centres and ends.

To make the pieced borders, start across the top and sew a main fabric half-triangle to a strip-pieced half-diamond, then a main fabric half-diamond. Continue in this manner until the row has four strip-pieced half-diamonds. Finish the row with a main fabric half-triangle. Pin then sew a 5¼ inch border fabric rectangle to each end. Match the centres and ends then pin and sew along the body of the quilt.

Repeat for the bottom pieced border. Next, assemble and attach the pieced side borders. One pieced side border starts with a half-triangle of main fabric, and the other with a stripped half-triangle. Both consist of 19 triangles sewn together along the diagonal, ending with a main fabric half-triangle. Make sure the main fabric triangles in the border align opposite those in the body of the quilt, as shown in the photograph.

Backing, quilting and binding

Measure your backing fabric and cut to fit, allowing a little extra, and piecing it if necessary to get the right size.

Refer to pages 192–197 for instructions on finishing.

This quilt was quilted in perle cotton No 8 in giant swirls, and outline-quilted around the designs in the inspiration fabric.

Strawberry Fields

Sarah Fielke   ADVANCED

THE IDEA

A lovely friend of mine from quilting died after a long battle with cancer. Not long before she died, she made a quilt using this block, which we helped her with in the shop. I loved it at the time and when she died I wanted to create a quilt using the block to remember her. I didn't have a pattern for it so it took a bit of trial and error to make it up. I had some special fabrics given to me by other friends that I had been saving for a special project and they were just right for this. When I look at the quilt, I think of Robyn and remember all the pretty quilts she made for her friends and family.

Instead of strawberries, you could choose some luscious florals to be showcased in the central stars.

Finished quilt size

King single, 150 x 226 cm (59 x 89 inches)
Finished block size: 10 inches square including seam allowance

Materials and tools

NOTE: *The pictured quilt was made using several linen fabrics, which are more loosely woven than patchwork cotton. If you are using linen, remember to cut and piece with care and not to handle the pieces too much, or they will stretch.*

65 cm (26 inches) big strawberry fabric for top and bottom border (fabric A)
80 cm (32 inches) white fabric (fabric B)
1.9 m (76 inches) red fabric with white spots (fabric C and binding)
30 cm (12 inches) white fabric with blue spots (fabric D)
20 cm (8 inches) white floral fabric (fabric E)
35 cm (14 inches) each of four different fabrics for frames (fabric F):
    Fabric F1 — multicoloured stripe
    Fabric F2 — white with green spots
    Fabric F3 — white with blue spots
    Fabric F4 — pink and blue floral
30 cm (12 inches) of each of 7–10 different large floral prints for the star centres (fabric G), or twenty 25 cm (10 inch) squares
Rotary cutter, ruler and mat
Cotton thread for piecing
4.9 m (5½ yds) backing fabric
170 x 245 cm (68 x 98 inch) piece cotton wadding
Perle cotton No 8 in pink, white and red for quilting (optional)

NOTE: *It is recommended that all fabrics be 100 percent cotton, and be ironed. Requirements are based on fabric 112 cm (44 inches) wide. Unless otherwise stated, all seam allowances are ¼ inch throughout. Colour test any dark fabrics that you are using (see page 177); if they run, wash them before cutting.*
    Please read all instructions before starting.

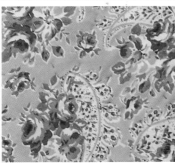

Cutting

FROM THE LARGE STRAWBERRY FABRIC (FABRIC A), cut three strips 8 inches wide. Cut one of these strips in half across the width.

FROM THE WHITE FABRIC (FABRIC B), CUT:
Eight strips 3¾ inches wide.
Cross cut one of these strips into four pieces 8½ inches long (B1).
Cross cut six of the strips into five pieces 7¾ inches long, giving a total of 30 pieces (B2).
Cross cut the remaining strip into four pieces 5¼ inches long (B3).

FROM THE RED AND WHITE SPOT FABRIC (FABRIC C), CUT:
Eight strips 2½ inches wide for binding and set aside.
Seven strips 3¼ inches wide. Cross cut these strips into eighty squares for the blocks.
Ten strips 2½ inches wide. Cross cut these strips into 160 squares for the sashing and borders.
Two strips 4 inches wide. Cross cut these strips into twelve squares, then cross cut on both diagonals to yield 48 triangles for the cornerstones.

FROM THE BLUE AND WHITE SPOT FABRIC (FABRIC D), cut three strips 3⅜ inches wide. Cross cut these strips into 24 squares. Cut these squares in half along one diagonal to form 48 half-square triangles for the cornerstones.

FROM THE WHITE FLORAL FABRIC (FABRIC E), cut two strips 3 inches wide. Cross cut these strips into twelve 3 inch squares for the cornerstones.

FROM EACH OF THE FOUR FRAME FABRICS (FABRIC F), cut four strips 3 inches wide from each fabric. Cross cut each strip into nine pieces 5¼ inches long, making a total of 124 pieces.

FROM THE LARGE FLORAL PRINTS (FABRIC G), cut twenty 10-inch squares.

Sewing

PIECING THE BLOCKS

1 For each fabric G square, take four 3-inch fabric C (red spot) squares. Fold the 3-inch squares in half diagonally and finger-press. Unfold, then align a 3-inch square with a corner of the G square, right sides together, so that the diagonal fold points touch two edges of the square (see Diagram 1). Sew along the fold mark, then cut the corners off ¼ inch outside the sewing line. Repeat for the other three corners of the square. Press the triangles out. Repeat for all twenty G blocks.

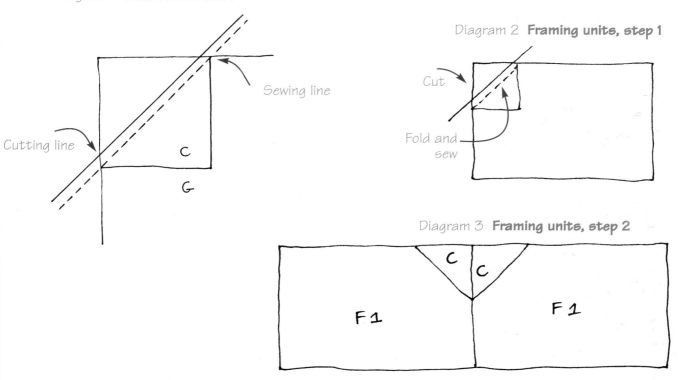

Diagram 1 **Star centre units**

Sewing line

Cutting line

C

G

Diagram 2 **Framing units, step 1**

Cut

Fold and sew

Diagram 3 **Framing units, step 2**

C

C

F 1

F 1

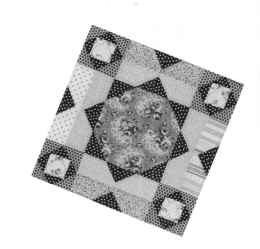

2 Using the four F fabrics in the same arrangement as shown in the photograph on page 153, you need 30 rectangles from two of the fabrics (F1 and F4), and 32 rectangles from the other two (F2 and F4). They will be joined in pairs as shown in Diagrams 2 and 3.

For each pair, take two 2¼ inch C squares, fold each in half diagonally, and finger press the diagonal line. Align a square, right sides together, with one corner of an F rectangle, so that the diagonal fold points touch two edges of the square. Sew along the fold line, then cut the point of the triangle off ¼ inch outside the sewing line (see Diagram 2). Press the triangle out. For the second piece of the pair, align the C square right sides together with the mirror-image corner of the F fabric piece, referring to Diagram 3 for placement. Cut and press as above, then sew the matching pairs together and press. You should have 62 matching pairs.

3 Assemble the cornerstone squares (see Diagram 4 on page 150). Take the twelve fabric E squares and sew one of the fabric C cornerstone triangles onto one side. Sew another to the opposite side of the square and press the triangles outwards. Cut the 'ears' off the triangles to reduce bulk, then repeat by sewing a triangle to the other two sides of the square. Press and trim the square if necessary.

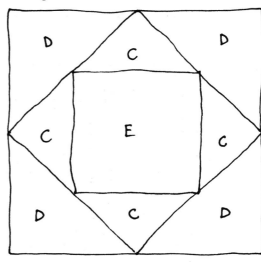

Diagram 4 **Cornerstones**

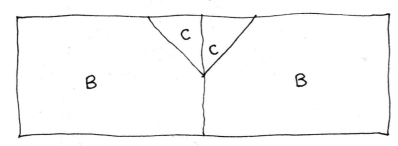

Diagram 5 **Border rectangles**

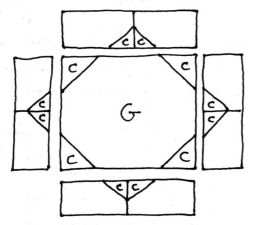

Diagram 6 **Star centres with F frames**

Now sew a fabric D triangle to two opposite sides of the square, and press out. Trim the ears again, then sew two more D triangles to the remaining two sides of the square and press. It should now measure 5½ inches square. Make 12 of these.

4 Make the B units for the first border by taking the remaining thirty-six 2½ inch C squares, folding in half diagonally and attaching to each B1 and B2 white rectangle in the same manner as for Step 2. Trim and press as before. Join together ten pairs of B2 rectangles with their triangles together in the centre as for the F blocks. See Diagram 5.

Join three of these B2 pairs together into a strip. Next join a B2 rectangle to each end, then a B3 rectangle to each end. Make sure the triangles are all along one edge and in pairs. This is one side border. Repeat these steps to make the other side border. Set aside.

5 Make the top and bottom borders in the same way, this time joining two pairs of B2 rectangles, then adding a B2 to either end, then a B1 rectangle to each end to finish the strip. Make two and set aside.

Construction

Arrange the main body of the quilt according to Diagram 7 and by rearranging the G centres and the various F frame pairs to your liking.

Sew the blocks into rows of four G blocks separated by the corresponding F pairs, then four blocks of F pairs joined into strips lengthwise. Take care to align the centre of the F pairs with the centre point of the G blocks, and trim the F pairs back if they are too long. Press.

Next, join the rows together. Again, when joining the rows of F pairs to the G blocks, be careful to align the centre seam of the F pairs to the centre point of the G squares.

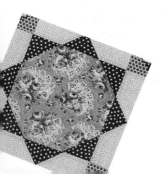

Diagram 7 **Quilt construction**

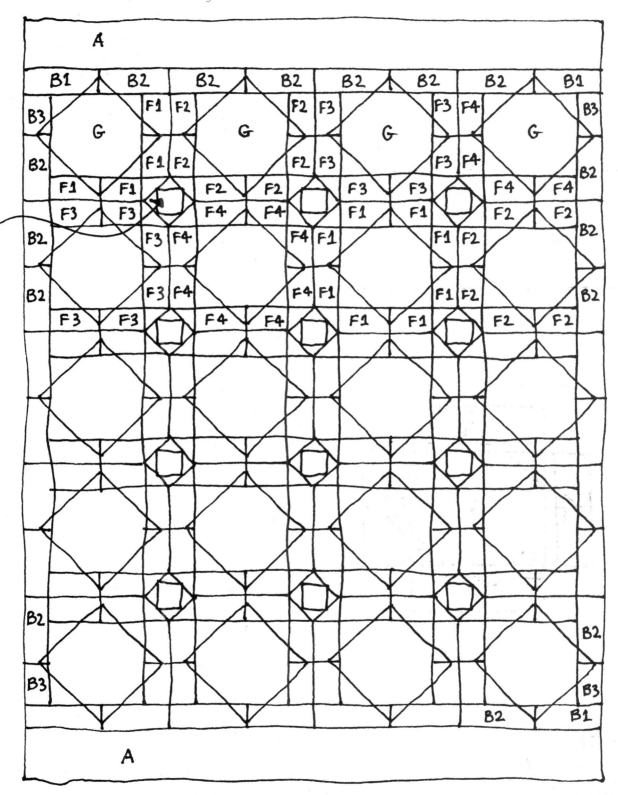

For the cornerstone squares, refer to Diagram 4

Borders

Join the white borders to the quilt centre. Find the centre of a white side border strip and the centre of the quilt body and finger-press a crease. Match these points and pin. Pin the ends together, then pin in between, easing as needed. This will minimise stretching. Sew the border on, then repeat with the other side border and press.

Now repeat these steps with the top and bottom white borders.

For the final top and bottom borders, measure the width of the quilt top. Join one long piece of strawberry fabric A to a short piece, press and trim to the width of the quilt top. Repeat with the remaining pieces of fabric A. Join one of these strips to the top and the other to the bottom of the quilt as detailed above.

Your quilt top is now complete. Press the entire quilt top carefully.

Backing, quilting and binding

Measure your backing fabric and cut to fit, allowing a little extra, and piecing it if necessary to get the right size.

Refer to pages 192–197 for instructions on finishing.

The blocks for this quilt were quilted in a star pattern using perle cotton No 8. The blocks were echo-quilted 1 inch apart using white, and hearts were quilted into the centre of the cornerstones with red cotton.

Liberty Fields

Kathy Doughty   ADVANCED

THE IDEA

One block from an antique quilt pictured in a diary — yellow Ohio Star blocks set on black with green stems — started this quilt. The diary sitting next to a stack of Liberty fabrics brought to mind the image of gorgeous flowers blowing in the wind.

This quilt also looks fantastic in small graphic prints in retro colours, or anything floral. The obvious choice is to go soft, but I'd love to think of it done in hot colours, or even as a two-colour quilt like the original, which was yellow and black.

Finished quilt size

Queen, 200 x 221 cm (79 x 87 inches)
Finished block size (single star): 8½ inches including seam allowance

Materials and tools

4.3 m (4¾ yards) quilter's muslin
5.3 m (6 yards) in total of up to 20 Liberty or other print fabrics, including
    12 inches (30 cm) green for the leaves
60 cm (24 inches) binding fabric
2.2 x 2.4 m (2½ x 2⅔ yards) piece cotton wadding
4.4 m (5 yards) backing fabric
Cardboard (card stock) and kitchen foil, for appliqué
2B pencil and sharpener
Rotary cutter, ruler and mat
Quarter-square triangle ruler and half-square ruler (optional)
Cotton thread for piecing
Green stranded embroidery cotton
Perle cotton No 8 in cream and an assortment of colours for the flowers

NOTE: *It is recommended that all fabrics be 100 percent cotton, and be ironed. Requirements are based on fabric 112 cm (44 inches) wide. Unless otherwise stated, all seam allowances are ¼ inch throughout. Colour test any dark fabrics that you are using (see page 177); if they run, wash them before cutting.*
    Please read all instructions before starting.

Preparation

Use the template provided to cut out the leaf shapes for the appliqué. To do this, trace the shapes onto cardboard using a sharp 2B pencil and cut out. Each template can be used several times; discard once the edges become worn. Trace the shape onto the back of the fabric. Cut out ¼ inch outside the line. Cut a piece of foil slightly larger than the fabric. Place the foil on an ironing board, then place the fabric on top, face down. Place the cardboard template on top of the fabric. Fold the foil around the edges

Diagram 1
(front of block)

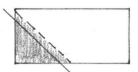

Diagram 2
(back of block) Trim ¼ inch
away from seam

Diagram 3
(front of block)

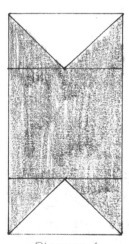

Diagram 4

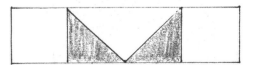

Diagram 5

and press with a hot iron. The heat will produce a neat fold that will be easy to appliqué.

Cutting

FROM THE QUILTER'S MUSLIN, CUT:

Two strips 8½ inches wide. Cross cut these into eight squares for the leaf/stem blocks.

Four strips 6½ inches wide. Cross cut into 20 squares for the pieced border.

Seven strips 4½ inches wide for the outer border.

Fifteen strips 2½ inches wide. Cross cut these into 136 rectangles 4½ inches wide for the base of the flower points.

Nine strips 2½ inches wide. Cross cut these into 136 squares for the cornerstones of the flower blocks.

One strip 8⅞ inches wide. Cross cut it into four squares, then cut these in half along one diagonal. Mark the pieces as quarter-square triangles and set aside for the tops and bottoms of the pieced borders.

Two strips 12 inches wide. Cross cut these into four squares. Cross cut the squares along both diagonals to produce four quarter-square triangles for setting the body of the quilt. **NOTE:** These triangles are cut larger than necessary in some cases; they will be trimmed back to square up the quilt before adding the borders.

FROM THE ASSORTED LIBERTY OR PRINT FABRICS, CUT:

Thirty-four 4½ inch squares for the centres of the flowers.

Seventeen strips 2½ inches wide. Cross cut these into 272 squares for the flower points.

Twenty-seven leaf shapes using the template provided (see page 158) and adding a ¼ inch seam allowance.

Thirty-four strips 2⅞ inches wide for the sashing squares. Pair these up, right sides together and raw edges even, cross cut into squares, then cut along one diagonal to make 270 sets of triangles for the sashing strips.

Assorted strips about 1½ x 4⅞ inches. Sew them together along the length to make four rows of strips 46¼ inches long. Cross cut them at 45-degree angles with a base (hypotenuse) measurement of 9¼ inches. Make the rows and cut them until you have 36 quarter-square triangles and four half-square triangles. The first and last cut in each row will be a half-square triangle. Mark eight for the tops and bottoms of each pieced border strip. The remaining cuts will reveal quarter-square triangles. We use this strip method to maintain the direction of the strips in the triangles.

Cut the remaining print fabrics into strips 1¾ inches wide and of varying lengths (no more than 3½ inches long) and sew them end to end for the top and bottom borders. When the body of the quilt is finished, measure the width and trim these strips to match.

Sewing

FLOWER BLOCKS

1 This is an Ohio Star block. Fold one 2½ inch Liberty square in half diagonally and finger press the crease. Match the corners and sew with the right sides together to the quilter's muslin rectangle along the diagonal crease (see Diagram 1). On the back of the unit, trim away excess fabric (see Diagram 2). Press open. Repeat for the right-hand side (see Diagram 3). Repeat for all four rectangles for all 34 stars.

2 Sew a rectangle from step 1 to the top and then another to the bottom of the main Liberty print square (see Diagram 4).

3 Sew a 2½ inch quilter's muslin square to both ends of the remaining units that you made in Step 1 (see Diagram 5). Pin the seams to match and attach these blocks to the main square (see Diagram 6). Press flat. Make 34 Ohio Star 'flowers' in this manner. Set aside ten flowers.

4 Group the remaining 24 flowers into eight sets of three. Sew two together by first matching and pinning the points. Sew an 8½ inch quilter's muslin square to the side of the third star block. Pin the centres and points and join both sets to form a square (see Diagram 7). Make eight units in this manner.

Embroidery and appliqué

On the quilter's muslin square, use a 2B pencil to lightly draw a single line from the bottom points of the stars to join with a single line forming the stem (see Diagram 8). The 'flow' of the stems on each block is different; see the photograph on page 161. Chain stitch along the line using two strands of green stranded cotton.

Decide where you want your leaf shapes to sit on the stems you have embroidered. Trace the leaf shape lightly onto the block using a 2B pencil. Using thread to match the colour of the leaf, appliqué the leaves to the muslin block (see Diagram 8). Use small stitches that just catch the edge of the fabric, and make extra stitches at the points of the leaves.

Sashing

The sashing comprises half-square triangles in the Liberty prints. Starting at the corner, sew the pairs of triangles together on the diagonal using a ¼ inch seam. Open and press flat. Sew these squares into six sets of four and six sets of five (these form the borders for the six outside single blocks); twelve sets of eight; two sets of ten; two sets of 28 squares; and one set of 37 squares.

Construction

The quilt is assembled as per Diagram 9 in diagonal rows starting in the top left-hand corner. The left-hand (upper) half of the quilt is made first,

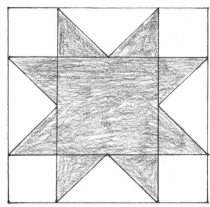

Diagram 6

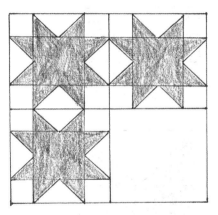

Diagram 7

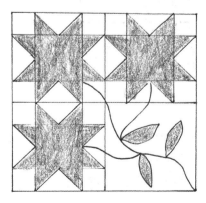

Diagram 8

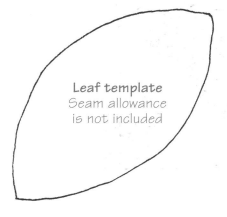

Leaf template
Seam allowance
is not included

then the right-hand (lower) half, then the two halves are joined diagonally to complete the quilt top.

CORNER FLOWER UNITS (MAKE 4)

Sew a quilter's muslin half-square triangle to two adjacent sides of each of four single flower blocks.

SINGLE FLOWER UNITS (MAKE 6)

Pin and sew a four-square sashing strip to one side of each of six single flower blocks. Then pin the points and sew a five-square sashing strip to an adjacent side. Sew a quilter's muslin quarter-square triangle to the two sashed sides of these sets.

BUNCHES OF FLOWERS

SINGLE–BUNCH UNITS (MAKE 2): Sew an eight-square sashing strip to opposite sides of two bunches of flowers. Sew a ten-square sashing strip to the top of one block and to the bottom of the other block. Pin then sew a single flower unit to both sides of each of these units. Refer to the diagram for placement and be sure the flowers are growing upward.

THREE–BUNCH UNITS (MAKE 2): Lay out three flower bunch blocks in a row (with the stems all growing upward). Alternating eight-square sashing strips and flower bunch blocks, and starting and ending with sashing strips, pin then sew to form a three-bunch block row.

Assembly

Sew a 28-square sashing strip to the top of one of the three-bunch units by matching up the sashing strips with the cross strips. Then sew a single flower unit to the bottom (left) end.

Matching up the cross strips, pin then sew the 37-square sashing strip to the bottom of this set.

Sew a corner flower unit to the top (right) end of this row.

Assemble this diagonal row with the single-bunch unit from above and the single corner unit to complete the top half of the quilt. Please note that the quarter-square muslin triangles on the side overlap where the diagonal rows are sewn together.

To make the bottom half of the quilt, proceed in a similar manner, starting in the bottom right corner and matching the centres and seams.

Sew a corner flower unit to the left end end of the second three-bunch unit and a single-flower unit to the right end.

Diagram 9 Quilt construction

Now the two ends of the quilt can be joined by matching all cross strips through the diagonal middle of the quilt.

Measure and note the width of the quilt. Trim the strips of Liberty rectangles to fit the measured width of the quilt. Match the middles and sew these strips to the top and bottom of the quilt.

The body of the quilt is now complete.

Borders

STRIP BORDERS

Start with two sets of 10 quilter's muslin squares.

Sew two half-square strip triangles to the top sides of two squares and the bottom sides of two squares. These will go at the ends of the borders.

Sew a quarter-square strip triangle to the top left-hand side of each of the remaining 16 squares, then sew a quarter-square triangle to the bottom right-hand side of the same squares.

Sew a quarter-square triangle to the bottom right-hand side of the top squares. Sew a quarter-square triangle to the top left-hand side of the bottom squares.

Working diagonally and matching seams, sew the squares together along the diagonal edges until you have two sets of 10 squares, starting and ending with half-square triangles.

Find the middle of the border strips and the middle of the body of the quilt. Match and pin the middles, then the ends, and then every few inches along the sides, easing as necessary. Sew in place and press flat.

PLAIN BORDERS

Measure the length through the centre of the quilt body.

Sew the quilter's muslin strips together, then cut them into two pieces equal to the length of the quilt. Find the middle of the border piece and the middle of the edge of the quilt body and finger-press a crease. Match these points and pin. Pin the ends, then pin in between, easing as necessary to make the two pieces fit together. Sew in place.

Measure the width of the quilt. Cut the remaining quilter's muslin strip into two pieces equal to the width (including the borders). Find the middle of the body of the quilt and the middle of the strips. Pin, then sew.

Backing, quilting and binding

Measure your backing fabric and cut to fit, allowing a little extra, and piecing it if necessary to get the right size.

Refer to pages 192–197 for instructions on finishing.

Perle cotton No 8 was used to quilt Liberty Fields in swirls and twists around the flower blocks and in the backgrounds. The flowers were quilted in matching colours in a variety of flowing patterns.

Surprise Package

Sarah Fielke   ADVANCED

THE IDEA

I bought an old, shabby quilt on Ebay for $9.95. It was made of polyester and not attractive, and the only reason I was interested in it was that the seller said briefly that it was lumpy, and she thought it might have been stuffed with an old quilt. That was enough to get my historic little heart racing, so I bid for it and won. I figured $9.95 wasn't a bad stake on a chance to see what was inside. When the quilt finally arrived I felt a bit foolish — it was really not nice, and what if there was nothing inside but rotten old cotton wadding? As soon as I cut the edge of the top, though, I knew I was on a winner. Surprise Package is my version of the 1930s Nosegay quilt I found inside.

A dark background would make a striking difference.

Finished quilt size

Throw or small cot size, 125 cm (49½ inches) square
Finished block size: 12½ inches square including seam allowance

Materials and tools

100 cm (40 inches) white linen or cotton fabric
60 cm (24 inches) pink spot fabric
30 cm (12 inches) green stripe fabric for bottom of Nosegay
10 cm (4 inches) of each of nine different fabrics for flower tops, or scraps
50 cm (20 inches) yellow spot fabric for cornerstones and binding
45 cm (18 inches) red and white stripe fabric for sashing
60 cm (24 inches) red and white patterned fabric for outer border
145 cm (58 inch) square piece wadding
3.1 m (3½ yds) backing fabric
Rotary cutter, ruler and mat
Template plastic
Scissors for template plastic
Quilter's quarter or other quarter-inch ruler
2B pencil and sharpener
Cotton thread for piecing
Off-white cotton for quilting

NOTE: *It is recommended that all fabric be 100 percent cotton, and be ironed. Requirements are based on fabric 112 cm (44 inches) wide. Unless otherwise stated, all seam allowances are ¼ inch throughout. Colour test any dark fabrics you are using (see page 177), and wash them before cutting if they run.*

We also recommend not pressing any part of the Nosegay blocks until they are complete. This prevents the bias edges on all the little triangles and odd-shaped bits from stretching out of shape and making your block wonky.

Diagram 1 **Unit 1** Make 18 (2 per block)

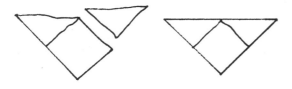

Diagram 2 **Unit 2** Make 27 (3 per block)

Diagram 3

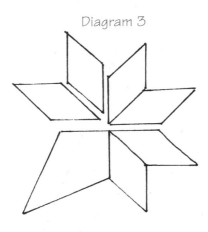

Diagram 4

Preparation

Trace each of the templates A–F onto the template plastic using a very sharp pencil and a ruler. Cut out one each of all the template pieces, and write their corresponding letters on them. Note that these templates include seam allowance. Trace around the templates using a sharp 2B pencil on the back of the fabric. Note also that Templates C and E are cut both right side up and reversed.

Cutting

FROM THE GREEN STRIPE FABRIC, cut nine of template A for the blocks. Be sure that the stripe runs in the direction that you want it to on each template.

FROM THE PINK SPOTTED FABRIC, cut 54 of template B.

FROM THE WHITE FABRIC, CUT:

Nine of template C, and nine of template C reversed.

36 of template D.

27 of template E, and 27 of template E reversed.

NOTE: *Make sure you keep the right side and reverse pieces in different stacks. A post-it note stuck to the top of the stacks is a good way to keep track, or you can put each stack in a labelled lock-top plastic bag.*

FROM THE ASSORTED COLOURED FABRICS, cut five of template F from each fabric (or a total of 45 pieces from scraps).

FROM THE RED STRIPE FABRIC, cut eight strips 2 inches wide. Cross cut these strips into 24 pieces 2 x 12½ inches for the sashing.

FROM THE RED AND WHITE BORDER FABRIC, cut six strips 3¾ inches wide.

FROM THE YELLOW SPOT FABRIC, CUT:

One strip 2 inches wide. Cross cut this strip to make sixteen squares for the cornerstones.

Six strips 2½ inches wide for the binding.

Sewing

NOSEGAY BLOCKS

Begin by making Unit 1. You will need two units for each block, eighteen in total. The unit is made by sewing a template D triangle to two adjacent sides of a template F square. Refer to Diagram 1 for placement, and be sure to trim the 'ears' off the triangles.

Using your quilter's quarter and a sharp 2B pencil, mark the quarter inch onto the back of the remaining template F squares and the template E pieces. To make Unit 2, first sew a template E piece to one side of a template F square. Stop sewing ¼ inch from the edge (t the point marked

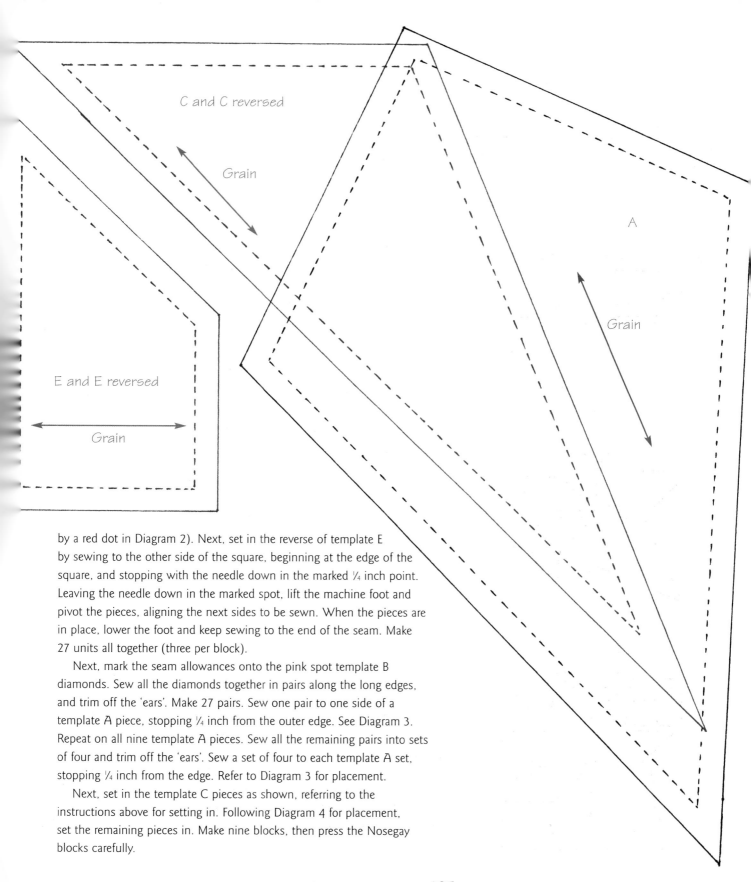

C and C reversed

Grain

E and E reversed

Grain

A

Grain

by a red dot in Diagram 2). Next, set in the reverse of template E by sewing to the other side of the square, beginning at the edge of the square, and stopping with the needle down in the marked ¼ inch point. Leaving the needle down in the marked spot, lift the machine foot and pivot the pieces, aligning the next sides to be sewn. When the pieces are in place, lower the foot and keep sewing to the end of the seam. Make 27 units all together (three per block).

Next, mark the seam allowances onto the pink spot template B diamonds. Sew all the diamonds together in pairs along the long edges, and trim off the 'ears'. Make 27 pairs. Sew one pair to one side of a template A piece, stopping ¼ inch from the outer edge. See Diagram 3. Repeat on all nine template A pieces. Sew all the remaining pairs into sets of four and trim off the 'ears'. Sew a set of four to each template A set, stopping ¼ inch from the edge. Refer to Diagram 3 for placement.

Next, set in the template C pieces as shown, referring to the instructions above for setting in. Following Diagram 4 for placement, set the remaining pieces in. Make nine blocks, then press the Nosegay blocks carefully.

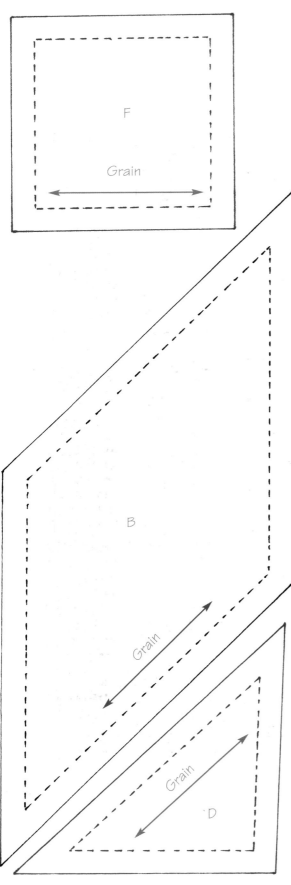

SASHING

Lay your Nosegay blocks out on the floor or a table and move them around until you are happy with the colour placement. Taking the first block of the first row, sew a sashing strip to either side, then sew the other two blocks in the row together separated by a sashing strip, creating a row that reads — sashing, block, sashing, block, sashing, block, sashing.

Repeat until you have pieced all three rows. Make the separating rows by making four strips that read thus: cornerstone, sashing, cornerstone, sashing, cornerstone, sashing, cornerstone.

Sew a sashing strip to the top of a block row, then a sashing strip to the bottom, alternating until you have sewn all the rows together, beginning and ending with a sashing strip. Press.

Borders

OUTER BORDER

Measure the size of your centre panel through the middle. Take the four border strips and carefully cut a 45-degree angle into one end of all four (see Diagram 5). You can use a half-square triangle ruler or the angles on a standard quilter's ruler for this. Measure out the length of the quilt from the bottom of the angled cut as shown, and then cut the other end of the strips in the opposite angle. Find the middle of one strip, and the middle of the centre panel, and pin together. Next pin the ends, then pin in between, easing as necessary. Sew the strip to the centre panel. Working around the quilt, sew the next border strip to the quilt, using the setting-in method to mitre the corners as you go. Press.

The quilt top is now complete. Press the entire quilt top carefully.

Backing, quilting and binding

Measure your backing fabric and cut to fit, allowing a little extra, and piecing it if necessary to get the right size.

Refer to pages 192–197 for instructions on finishing.

Surprise Package was quilted using traditional waxed quilting thread to echo quilt around each block, ¼ inch apart over the whole block. The quilting lines were marked out with ¼ inch masking tape.

Diagram 5 **Measuring and cutting borders**

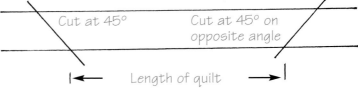

Stripping Vine

Kathy Doughty   ADVANCED

THE IDEA

Sometimes fabric begs not to be cut up. The instant I saw this Valorie Wells vine fabric I knew what had to be done — it had to be cut in long strips to make a strong impact. This fabric is rather subdued and moody in tone. To go with it, I mixed lots of bits from my stash that were in the autumn tones of the fabric, including Kaffe Fassett fabrics, Japanese, tie-dye and even Civil War reproductions.

Patterns that flow along the length of the bolt are great for this quilt. Buy the length of the quilt you want to make and cut it along the length. Hang it on the wall, then start making the smaller star blocks.

Finished quilt size

Queen, 224 x 230 cm (88 x 90 inches)

Materials and tools

2.25 m (2½ yds) main fabric for strips
2 m (2¼ yds) fabric for setting triangles
20 cm (8 inches) of each of 10 fabrics for the star centres, or use a variety of fabrics 17 cm (6½ inches) square
50 cm (20 inches) in total for inner star points
50 cm (20 inches) in total for outer star points
1.35 m (1½ yds) in total for cornerstones and packing rectangles (or five 30 cm/12 inch pieces)
60 cm (24 inches) binding fabric
7.2 m (8 yards) backing fabric; or use 2.5 m (2¾ yards) of 250 cm (100 inch) wide backing fabric
240 x 265 cm (96 x 106 inch) piece of cotton wadding
Neutral-coloured cotton for piecing
Rotary cutter, ruler and mat and optional Creative Grids 45-degree ruler
Four balls perle cotton No 8 for quilting

NOTE: *It is recommended that all fabrics be 100 percent cotton, and be ironed. Requirements are based on fabric 112 cm (44 inches) wide. Unless otherwise stated, all seam allowances are ¼ inch throughout. Colour test any dark fabrics that you are using (see page 177); if they run, wash them before cutting.*
Please read all instructions before starting.

Cutting

FOLD THE MAIN FABRIC IN HALF and then in half again along the length of the piece (2.25 m/2½ yds), being most careful to get the folds flat and the grain as straight as possible. Cut the selvedges off and then cut the fabric into four equal strips 25 cm (10 inches) wide by the length of the fabric. Set aside.

Diagram 1
(front of block)

Diagram 2
(back of block) Trim
¼ inch away from seam

Diagram 3
(front of block)

Diagram 4   Diagram 5

Diagram 6

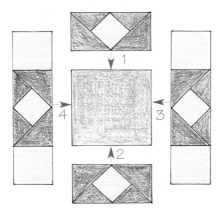

Diagram 7

Diagram 8

FROM THE FABRIC FOR THE SETTING TRIANGLES, CUT:

Three strips 18¼ inches wide. Cross cut these into six squares. Cut through the squares along both diagonals to form four triangles from each square (a total of 24 triangles). These quarter-square triangles are for the sides of the star block strips; label and set aside.

Two strips 9⅜ inches wide. Cross cut these into six squares. Cut through these squares along one diagonal to form two triangles from each square (a total of 12 triangles). These half-square triangles are for the corners of the star block strips; label and set aside.

FROM THE STAR CENTRE FABRICS, CUT:

Fifteen 6½ inch squares.

Fifteen strips 3½ inches wide in light colours. From these, cross cut 60 cornerstones 3½ inches square and 60 rectangles 3½ x 6½ inches.

Select two contrasting colours for the star points of each block. Go wild with your combinations and have fun! Each of the 15 blocks will need eight 3½ inch squares for the inner star points and eight for the outer star points.

FROM THE BINDING FABRIC, cut strips 2½ inches wide.

Sewing

Start by establishing your block sets. Lay out your colour groupings in sets of one star centre block, four rectangles, four cornerstones, eight inner star points and eight outer star points.

1 Take one 3½ x 6½ inch rectangle and two 3½ inch squares. Fold each square in half diagonally and finger-press. Line up one square with one end of the rectangle, right sides together (see Diagram 1). Unfold, then sew along the fold line.

Turn the unit over and cut off the outside triangles of both fabrics, ¼ inch beyond the sewing line (see Diagram 2). Fold the triangle back into place and press the seam toward the darker fabric.

Repeat this process on the other side of the rectangle with the second square (see Diagram 3). Make 4 for each block.

2 Take two contrasting 3½ inch squares and repeat the above process in the opposite direction on each of the four rectangles (see Diagrams 4 and 5).

3 Sew a cornerstone to each end of two 3½ x 6½ inch rectangles (see Diagram 6).

4 Sew the other two rectangles to the top and bottom of the centre square (see Diagram 7). Sew the rectangle-and-cornerstone units that you made in the previous step to this piece, matching the corner points carefully. The Double Ohio Star block is now finished (see Diagram 8).

Each block should measure 12 inches finished. Make 15 blocks.

Diagram 9
Block row construction

Setting triangles

1 Before sewing any seams, lay out the stars for placement in three rows of five on a design wall or a large flat space. Stand back and view the placement, being mindful of colour and texture balance. Look through the lens of a camera to get a more concentrated view of the quilt, or simply squint at it to get an idea of the tonal balance. Check that stripes are going in the intended direction, that stars containing similar fabrics are well spaced apart and that light and dark stars balance throughout the quilt. Any inconsistencies in sizing need to be trimmed at this time.

2 Set the stars by starting at the top of each row and working diagonally through the strip. (See Diagram 9; the numbered arrows refer to the order in which the components are pieced. The components for one diagonal row are joined first, then those for the next row, then the two rows are sewn together.) Sew a small half-square corner triangle to the top left-hand and right-hand sides of the star. Sew a large quarter-square setting triangle to the bottom right-hand side of the square. The next quarter-square triangle is sewn to the top of the next star block and then the opposite end. Line up these two sets and pin all points carefully before sewing them together. Finish the end of the row with two small half-square triangles. Make three rows of five.

3 Fold the main strips and rows of stars in half lengthwise and finger-press a crease to mark. Match these points and pin. Pin the ends, then pin along the rest of the seam, easing as necessary. Sew together.

Repeat with the other main strips and rows of stars, alternating them, to complete the quilt top (refer to the photograph on page 173).

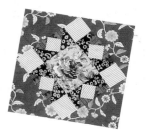

Backing, quilting and binding

If you are using 112 cm (44 inch) wide backing fabric, remove the selvedges from the fabric, cut widthwise into three pieces each 2.4 m (95 inches) long and sew them together along the length (what was previously the selvedges) to form a backing piece large enough.

If you are using 200-inch wide backing fabric, you will not need to piece it; simply remove the selvedges.

Refer to pages 192–197 for instructions on finishing.

Stripping Vine was quilted with perle cotton No 8. In the strips the quilting repeats the design of the fabric, and in the stars it is ¼ inch from the seams.

quilting basics

Some waddings need to be quilted closer together than others to stop them from drifting around within the quilt or fragmenting when washed.

Polyester wadding requires less quilting than cotton or wool wadding. However, some polyester waddings have a tendency to 'fight' the sewing machine.

Wool waddings (usually actually a wool/polyester or a wool/cotton blend) provide more warmth and comfort than polyester waddings. However, they require more quilting, and those that are not needle-punched tend to pill. Needle-punched wool blends are more stable and require less quilting.

Traditional cotton waddings require a lot of quilting, as much as every ½–3 inches (12–75 mm). Needle-punched cotton waddings are more stable and can be quilted up to 10 inches (25 cm) apart.

THE PARTS OF A QUILT

Most quilts consists of three layers: the quilt top (the decorative part); the wadding (the filling, which provides warmth and also contributes to the padded look of the quilt); and the quilt backing. The wadding may be omitted if you want a very light quilt for summer, or if the fabrics used in the quilt top and backing are heavy enough on their own. The edges of the quilt are finished with binding.

THE QUILT TOP generally consists of a central design or a series of blocks surrounded by one or more borders, and may be pieced (made of patchwork) or appliquéd (with designs sewn onto a background). Whole-cloth quilts are those with a top made entirely of one (usually plain) fabric; these provide the most effective background for very intricate quilting patterns.

WADDING (also known as batting) is the quilt's filling. It may be made of wool, cotton, polyester or a mixture of these; each has different properties (see left). Cotton and wool are easier to quilt than polyester.

THE QUILT BACKING is usually made of one fabric, but it can be made wholly or partly from leftover patchwork blocks, or strips or fat quarters of different fabrics. If using just the one fabric in the standard 44 inch (112 cm) width, you will normally need to join two lengths to create a backing wide enough for anything larger than a cot or lap quilt. It is possible to buy backing fabrics in wider widths so as to avoid having to piece the backing. Use a good-quality fabric; poor-quality backing can result in uneven wear and ruin all your hard work.

BINDING finishes the raw edges of all layers of the quilt by enclosing them in a thin strip of fabric. Binding is generally made from a double thickness of fabric for extra durability, as the edges of a quilt will wear more quickly than other parts. Binding is the last thing to be done, once the quilting is finished.

FABRIC FOR QUILTS

For most quilts, it is best to use pure cotton fabrics. These wash and iron well, are easy to sew, take a crease well and do not fray excessively. Generally, all fabrics used for a quilt should be of a similar weight and weave. Using fabrics of different weights may result in some areas of the quilt wearing more quickly than others.

Fabric can be solid (a uniform colour, without a print or pattern); printed; tone-on-tone (having a background printed with a design of the same colour); or checked. Printed fabrics may have small, medium, large or directional prints. Small prints may look almost like solid fabrics from a distance. Medium prints are more distinct and are often used to add visual texture. Large prints have very distinct patterns that stand out from the background, and are often used in quilts as borders or feature prints. Directional prints have a very distinct pattern that runs in one direction. They can be particularly effective when used in a border or in a strippy quilt, such as Stripping Vine (page 166).

When choosing fabrics, think about both the balance of prints and plains as well as the tonal values of the fabrics; that is, the mixture of light, medium and dark fabrics. You will also find that the effect of a fabric may change according to the various values of the other fabrics surrounding it, with often surprising results. Experimenting with colour, tone and pattern is one of the pleasures of quilting.

Fabric grain

Fabric has three grains. The lengthwise grain runs the length of the fabric from top to bottom. The cross grain runs the width of the fabric, from selvedge to selvedge. Both the lengthwise and cross grains are straight grains. The bias grain runs at a 45-degree angle to the straight of the grain.

When cutting fabrics, most instructions and templates will tell you to cut on the straight of the grain. Rotary-cut strips are usually cut on the cross grain. An arrow on the template or pattern piece shows you the direction in which the grain should run when cutting out the fabric.

Cutting fabric on the bias will cause the cut edges to stretch; this is undesirable when piecing, although sometimes unavoidable (as when working with triangles). Where bias occurs, it is important to contain it within the quilt rather than having it along the outer edges, as it is difficult to achieve a neat finish to when applying borders and bindings to wavy, bias-cut edges. However, bias can be useful if you need to make the fabric curve, as when making bindings for a quilt with a curved border or when making bias strips for curved sections of appliqué.

PREPARING FABRICS

Many quilters prefer to wash, dry and iron cotton quilt fabrics before use. Wash each fabric separately in warm water with a scrap of white cotton fabric to test if the colour runs. If it does, the fabric should be discarded or used for another purpose. Otherwise, when the quilt is washed, the colour may run and ruin the quilt.

Washing pre-shrinks fabric and removes all finishes added by the manufacturer. Such finishes can make the fabric stiffer and easier to sew; if you wish to restore the stiffness, spray the fabric lightly with spray starch before sewing.

Before sewing, remove the tightly woven edges (selvedges) from all fabrics. These shrink at a different rate from the rest of the fabric, so if they are left on and included in seams, they may cause the fabric to pucker and bunch when it is laundered.

Above left: Choose threads to match your fabrics. For appliqué, special short appliqué pins are best (see page 180). **Far left:** A colour wheel can help in choosing contrasting and complementary colours. **Left:** Each of these three piles of fabrics works well due to the differing colours, tones and scales of print.

CHOOSING THREADS

Match the thread to the fabric when piecing; for example, when using cotton fabric, use cotton thread. Avoid using polyester thread with a cotton fabric; over time it will cut through the fibres of the cotton.

In most situations, cream, white or grey threads are appropriate for piecing. If using a multicoloured fabric, use a neutral thread, such as grey or beige, to match the tone of the background.

The same rule applies when choosing thread for machine quilting. Monofilament thread, which is transparent, is the most appropriate thread for quilt tops, as it takes on the colour of any fabric with which it is used. Although made of nylon, monofilament thread has the elastic quality of cotton.

Monofilament thread should be used as the top thread in the machine. In the bobbin, use a quilting thread that matches the backing fabric. The top tension in the machine should be eased off so that the heavier quilting thread will anchor the quilting stitches in the wadding.

When machine-piecing, use a stitch length of about 2.5, to produce 12–14 stitches per inch (2.5 cm).

EQUIPMENT

Not all of the items listed below are essential; some simply make the work easier. The quilts in this book are pieced by machine, but can be adapted for hand piecing.

Sewing machine and accessories

For the projects in this book, you will need a sewing machine in good working order that is capable of straight stitch. Before you start sewing, clean out the machine's bobbin with a brush or a lint-free cloth, and oil the machine, if it needs it. Insert a new needle; a dull needle can prevent stitches from forming properly.

SEWING MACHINE FEET AND NEEDLES

For piecing, you need a foot that gives you an accurate ¼ inch seam. Most patchwork uses the imperial system rather than metric (see page 183), but most sewing machine dealers will be able to provide an accurate ¼ inch foot. For older machines, there are feet that can be adapted.

If you cannot acquire a ¼ inch foot, place a ruler under the machine's needle and mark ¼ inch from the needle to the right, then draw a vertical line at this point with a pen, or mark it off with masking tape. Make sure the seam is accurate by sewing pieces together and then measuring the seam before starting a project.

For machine quilting, you will need a walking foot and a darning foot. A walking foot is used for all straight-line quilting. It allows layers of fabric to move through the machine without shifting. A darning foot is used to do free-motion quilting by dropping the feed dogs so that you can manoeuvre the quilt in any direction.

For general piecing, the best needle sizes to use for cotton fabrics are sizes 70/10 and 80/12. For machine quilting, use a size 75/11 quilting needle for thin and/or natural wadding quilts and a size 90/14 quilting needle for quilts with high-loft and/or polyester wadding.

Rotary cutting equipment

Rotary cutting makes it easy to cut fabrics quickly and accurately. Several layers of fabric can be cut at once.

ROTARY CUTTERS

A rotary cutter is a round, razor-sharp blade attached to a handle, protected by a sheath. Many styles of cutter are available. The standard size blade is 1¾ inches (45 mm). This is suitable for most cutting tasks, but for cutting through multiple layers, a 2⅜ inch (60 mm) or 2½ inch (65 mm) blade gives best results. A cutter with a blade this size is also easier to hold.

When you are holding a rotary cutter, the handle should rest comfortably in the palm and the index finger or thumb should be placed on the top edge of the cutter handle. There is usually a ridged section in this area to help provide grip. The blade side of the cutter should face the body and cuts should be made away from the body, using a smooth, firm, continuous motion.

ROTARY CUTTING MATS

A cutting mat should be used with a rotary cutter to protect both the blade of the rotary cutter and the work surface. Rotary cutting mats are made from self-healing plastic that allows cuts to mend. The size of the cutting mat depends on the size of the work area, but the mat should be able to accommodate a quarter of the width of the fabric (approximately 11 inches/28 cm). The bigger the mat, the longer the cut you will be able to make. Rotary cutting mats should be placed on a firm surface, stored flat and kept away from heat, which causes them to warp.

ROTARY CUTTING RULERS

Rotary cutting rulers (sometimes called quilter's rulers) are made of acrylic and are transparent. Designed to be used in conjunction with rotary cutters and mats, they have markings at ⅛ inch intervals. To make the quilts in this book, you will need a 6½ x 24 inch ruler. It is also handy to have another ruler the same size to assist in cutting strips without having to turn the cutting mat around (see page 182). A smaller ruler (6½ x 12 inches) is useful for cutting smaller strips of fabric.

Always measure and cut using the lines on the ruler rather than those on the cutting mat; if you cut too many times along the same lines on the mat, you will both damage the mat and erase or blur the lines, making them inaccurate.

Square rulers, which come in various sizes, are handy but not essential. The larger sizes make it possible to cut large squares in one movement. The smaller square rulers are good for cutting small pieces of fabric and for trimming up.

Other rulers are available to help you to cut fabric at various angles; these are useful for cutting half-square or quarter-square triangles, diamonds or wedge-shaped pieces, as used in Ginger Snap (page 140), Dotty for Dresden (page 120) and Three-ring Circus (page 128). See pages 185–187 for more information.

ROTARY CUTTER SAFETY HINTS

Safety should be a priority when using the rotary cutter. The blade should be exposed only when a cut is to be made (this can be done with the thumb) and the protective sheath should be replaced as soon as the cut is finished to protect you and to prevent the blade from being damaged.

Never leave rotary cutters lying about where they can be found by children or pets. A rotary cutter is essentially a circular razor blade, so treat it accordingly.

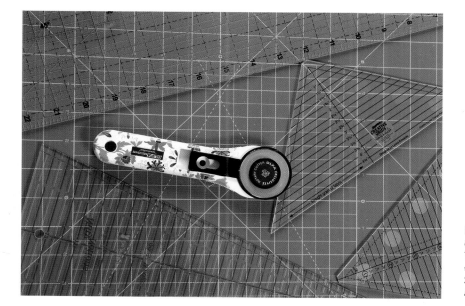

Left: Rotary cutting equipment on a rotary cutting mat. In the centre is a rotary cutter. The rulers, clockwise from top left, are a standard quilter's ruler measuring 6½ x 24 inches; a quarter-square triangle ruler; a 60-degree ruler; and a wedge ruler.

TEMPLATES AND TEMPLATE PLASTIC

Transparent template plastic is used to trace shapes onto fabric in much the same way as cardboard templates. The advantage of template plastic is that it is much more durable than cardboard, so it can be drawn around numerous times without the shape becoming distorted. It comes in plain and grid versions.

To use template plastic to create a fabric shape, trace the template onto the plastic using a pencil then cut it out with a craft knife or paper scissors.

Commercial templates, made of rigid plastic, are also available. They come in various shapes and sizes. They are durable, so they can be used over and over again, and are very precisely cut to give greater accuracy.

See pages 188–189 for more information on cutting and using templates.

Accessories

PINS

Long, fine pins with heads that lie flat against the fabric are recommended, as they will go through layers of fabric easily, and allow you to sew up to and over them without the stitching puckering. Fine pins are preferable, as thick, large pins cause the fabric to bunch up and the piecing to be inaccurate. Pins should be placed at right angles to seams. For appliqué, special appliqué and sequin pins are available; they are very short (½ inch/8 mm) to prevent the thread from becoming caught around the appliqué pieces as you sew them down.

SCISSORS

You will need a pair of fabric shears or a large pair of scissors to use exclusively to cut fabric; thread clips or small scissors to clip threads when sewing; and a pair of scissors to cut templates from plastic and paper. Don't use the same scissors for fabric and paper, as the paper will make them too blunt to cut fabric easily.

USEFUL BITS AND PIECES

There are various small accessories available to make patchwork and quilting easier, including:

ERASABLE PENCILS are used for tracing quilting designs that can later be erased onto the quilt top. Some pencils are also water soluble.

QUILTER'S QUARTERS are perspex rods ¼ inch square and about 12 inches (30 cm) long, used for tracing precise ¼ inch seams along the straight edge of a template.

THIMBLES come in two types, leather and metal. Leather ones can be used on the fingers of the underneath hand when quilting, to prevent the needle constantly pricking the finger when it is pushed to the underside of the quilt. A metal thimble is used on the middle finger of the upper hand to push the needle through all the layers of the quilt.

FUSIBLE INTERFACING is useful for stabilising fine or slippery fabrics, or those that fray easily, before piecing. It is also used for appliqué. It may be fusible on one side only, or both. When using double-sided fusible interfacing (such as Vliesofix), one side is ironed onto the back of the appliqué fabric, the shape is then cut out, the backing paper peeled off and the fabric piece ironed onto the right side of the background fabric.

CUTTING FABRIC

When cutting fabric, accuracy is essential to ensure that the individual components will align exactly and the finished quilt will be the correct size. Rotary cutting is suitable for geometric shapes; curved shapes will need to be cut by hand.

Rotary-cutting strips

To prepare fabric for cutting strips using a rotary cutter, first iron the fabric flat. Fold the fabric in half along its length, and do this again, so that you have four layers. Make sure you fold along the warp threads (the threads that run down the fabric, parallel to the selvedges). This may mean that the selvedges do not align.

Lay the folded fabric on a rotary cutter mat with the raw edge to the right if you are right-handed, to the left if you are left-handed. The folds will now be at a horizontal position. Place a quilter's ruler over the fabric, at right angles to the folds (see photograph below left), hold it firmly in place, and trim the raw edges with a rotary cutter. Unfold the piece you have cut off and check the angle of the cut; it must be dead straight, with no kinks at the folds. If not, refold the fabric and try again until the cut is straight.

Below left: *Aligning the fold of the fabric with the ruler before making the first cut, which will even up the raw edges of the fabric and establish a straight edge.* **Below right:** *Aligning fabric and two rulers, ready to cut the first strip.* **Bottom left:** *Cutting the first strip.* **Bottom right:** *One strip has been cut, and the fabric and rulers are in place ready to cut the next strip.*

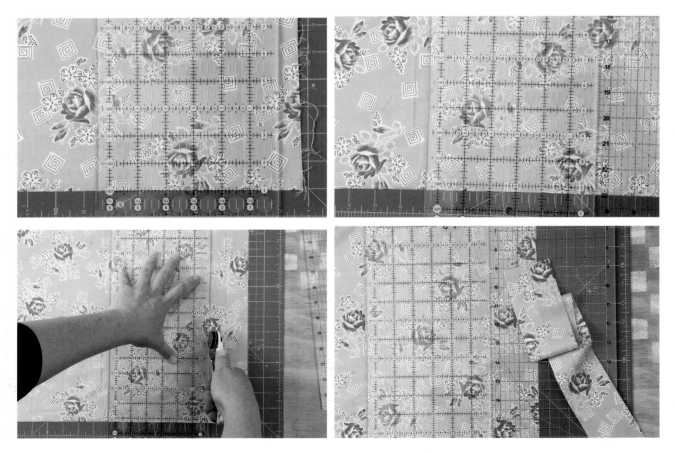

Now align the appropriate markings on the ruler with the edge you have just cut (for example, if you wish to cut a 2½ inch strip as in the photographs opposite, align the 2½ inch mark on the ruler with the cut edge of the fabric). Now take another ruler of the same length and butt it up against the edge of the first ruler, making sure that the first ruler does not move (if it does, realign it to the correct measurements). Move the first ruler to one side and cut using the edge of the second ruler as your guide. This method saves you having to turn the fabric and the cutting mat 180 degrees to avoid having to cut the fabric with your non-dominant hand.

Rotary-cutting squares or rectangles from strips

Once you have cut strips, you can cross cut them into squares or other shapes. The seam allowance will need to be calculated in your measurements.

To calculate the measurement for a square, add ½ inch for the seam allowance to the finished size of the square. To cut a square from a strip, open the strip to a double thickness only. Trim the selvedge. Cut to the same measurement that you used to cut the strip. To check that the measurement is correct, align the 45-degree mark on the quilter's ruler with the corner edge of the strip. If it runs through the opposite diagonal corner, it is correct. Every third or fourth cut, realign the cut edge.

To cut a rectangle from a strip, repeat the procedure for a square, remembering to add ½ inch to the finished measurement for the seam allowance.

A NOTE ON MEASUREMENTS

Measurements for patchwork and quilting are traditionally given in imperial units. This is still generally the case even in countries that have long used the metric system.

Many quilting accessories, such as rotary cutting mats and quilter's rulers, give measurements only in imperial. For the quilts in this book, imperial measurements are given in the cutting and sewing instructions, but fabric requirements are given in both metric and imperial.

Below left: Making the first cut, to trim off the raw edges. Here, three layers of fabric are being cut at once. **Below centre:** After the first strip has been cut from the width of the fabric, the selvedges are cut off. **Below right:** Cross cutting a strip to make squares. Here, the strips and squares are cut to 6½ inches (the width of the ruler).

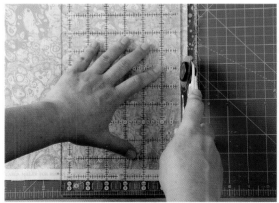
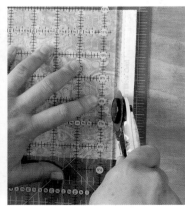
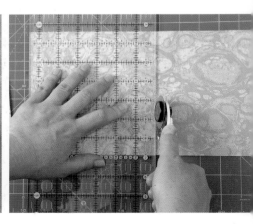

Rotary-cutting triangles

To save time and increase accuracy, triangles can be cut from strips, using either a standard quilter's ruler or specialised rulers. Each method requires a different initial measurement for the strips; both are explained below.

USING A STANDARD QUILTER'S RULER

To cut half-square triangles from a strip, using a standard quilter's ruler, calculate the finished size of the block required and add a $7/8$ inch seam allowance. Cut strips and then squares to this measurement. Cut once on the diagonal from corner to corner. Each square will yield two triangles.

To cut quarter-square triangles from a strip, using a standard quilter's ruler, calculate the finished size of the block required, and add a $1\frac{1}{4}$ inch seam allowance. Cut strips and then squares to this measurement. Cut twice on the diagonal from corner to corner. Each square will yield four triangles.

NOTE: *It is generally better to sew along the straight grain of a cut piece, as this prevents stretching, which can happen if you sew along a bias edge. Keep this in mind when you are cutting triangles. Half-square triangles have the straight of the grain along their two right-angled sides. Quarter-square triangles have the straight of the grain along the hypotenuse.*

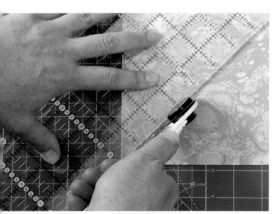

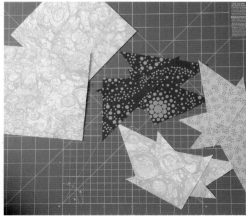

Above: Cross cutting a square along one diagonal to make half-square triangles. **Right:** To make quarter-square triangles, leave the pieces from the previous step undisturbed on the cutting mat, and cut across the second diagonal. **Far right:** Uncut squares and the quarter-square triangles that were made from them. Here, three fabrics were cut at once.

USING SPECIALISED RULERS

Special rulers are available to help you cut either half-square or quarter-square triangles. These rulers have done the mathematics for you. Simply cut strips as you would for squares. The rulers have blunt points that allow for the seam allowance at the point of the triangle, eliminating 'ears'. Calculate the finished size of the triangle required and add ½ inch for the seam allowance. Cut strips to this measurement and establish a straight edge.

To cut half-square triangles, align the ¼ inch mark at the narrow end of the half-square ruler with the top of the cut edge of the strip. Align the edge of the ruler with the cut end of the strip and the blunt point at the top, ensuring that the measurement markings line up flush with the bottom of the strip. Cut the first triangle along the diagonal edge of the ruler. Flip the ruler, this time placing it so that the ¼ inch mark at the narrow end of the ruler aligns with the lower cut edge of the strip. Cut the second triangle along the straight edge of the ruler. Repeat along the length of the strip.

QUARTER–SQUARE TRIANGLES

Align the point of the ruler with the upper cut edge of the fabric and cut along both diagonal edges of the ruler. Flip the ruler so that its point aligns with the bottom cut edge of the fabric, and the left edge of the ruler with the left cut edge of the fabric strip. Cut along the right diagonal edge of the ruler to create the second triangle.

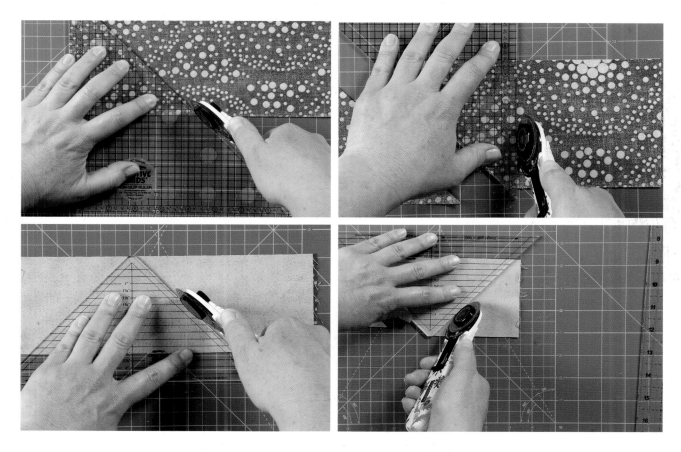

Top left: Using a half-square ruler to cut half-square triangles from a strip. The first cut is made along the diagonal edge of the ruler. **Top right:** The ruler is flipped and the second cut is made along the straight edge. **Above:** Using a quarter-square ruler to cut quarter-square triangles. The first cuts are made along both diagonal edges of the ruler. **Above right:** The ruler is flipped and a second diagonal cut is made as shown.

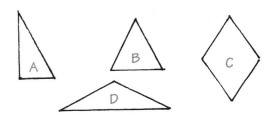

60-degree cutting

Using a specialised 60-degree ruler makes it easy to cut a variety of shapes (see Diagram 1), such as diamonds (Shape C), half-diamonds (Shape D), and 60-degree triangles (Shape B) and half-triangles (Shape A). These shapes are used in two of the quilts in this book (Ginger Snap, page 140, and Three-ring Circus, page 128). Cutting shapes in this way saves time, increases accuracy and makes economical use of the fabrics.

The following diagrams show various cutting layouts from strips and the number of each shape that can be produced in each case.

The diagrams and instructions here are for here shapes cut from an 8½ inch strip, as used in Ginger Snap (page 140). To determine fabric requirements for other sizes, measure the width of the shape at the base, add the width of the blunt edge and divide the width of the fabric by this amount.

Be mindful that when cutting A and D shapes, the cutting line is to the left or right of centre on the ruler so as to allow for the seam allowance. The centre line is the sewing line in both cases.

CUTTING TRIANGLES AND HALF-TRIANGLES

First, cut a strip ½ inch wider than the finished size of the shape; for example, if you want an 8 inch triangle, cut strips 8½ inches wide. More than one fabric can be cut at once. Then cross cut the strips using the 60-degree ruler. In the illustrated example (Diagram 2), the first and last cuts will yield a half-triangle. Flip the ruler to cut triangles from the middle of the strip as shown.

CUTTING TRIANGLES, HALF-TRIANGLES, DIAMONDS AND HALF-DIAMONDS

Establish a straight edge at the right end. Unfold to a single layer. Place the pointed end of the ruler at the bottom of the right-hand end of the strip and the base of

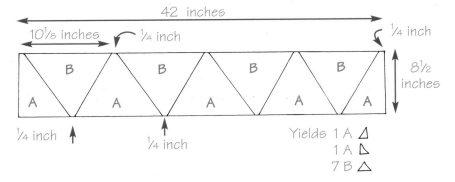

Diagram 2
Cutting triangles and
half-triangles from strips

42 inches

10⅛ inches   ¼ inch   ¼ inch

8½ inches

¼ inch   ¼ inch

Yields 1 A
1 A
7 B

the ruler at the top, with the dotted line to the right of centre on the straight end. Place a second ruler against the 60-degree ruler and cut along the diagonal edge of the second ruler after removing the 60-degree ruler. The cut-away piece is a half-triangle (shape A).

Measure 10⅛ inches from the right bottom to the left, mark with a pencil and do the same for the top. Use the 60-degree ruler (or the 60-degree line on your straight ruler) and cut a diagonal line between the points. Repeat twice to create three diamonds (shape C). When these are cut, fold them in half with a fold at the widest point. Use the ruler to trim to the exact shape, with the 8¼ inch line resting on the fold of the diamond. The remaining fabric in this strip will yield a triangle (Shape B).

Cut three strips 5¼ inches wide. Establish a straight edge on both ends of the strip. Use a previously cut half-triangle as a guide and cut along the diagonal from the right end of the strip. Cut away the half-triangle and fold the pointed end until the ruler fits to cut a half-diamond (Shape D). The dotted line to the left of the centre will line up with the bottom of the strip, and the 8¼ inch line will line up with the folded end. Cut along the diagonal and repeat until there are four half-diamonds. End with a half-triangle.

CREATING HEXAGONS

Hexagons are easily made from sets of six 60-degree triangles. (These add up to 360 degrees, making a circle.) First create a half-hexagon by sewing together three triangles as shown below (Diagram 5). Create another half-hexagon in the same way.

The hexagon can be joined in one of two ways. The first is simply to sew the two halves across the middle, taking care to match the points in the centre. This is the method used in Three-ring Circus (page 128). In the other method, the half-hexagons are joined to other shapes (for example triangles or diamonds) in horizontal rows. When these rows are joined, whole hexagons are formed. This is the method used in Ginger Snap (page 140).

Diagram 3
Cutting diamonds, triangles and half-triangles from strips

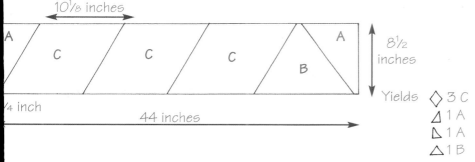

10⅛ inches

8½ inches

44 inches

¼ inch

Yields ◇ 3 C
△ 1 A
◺ 1 A
△ 1 B

Diagram 4
Cutting half-diamonds and half-triangles from strips

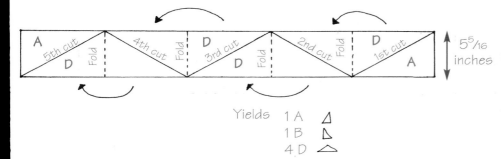

5⁵⁄₁₆ inches

Yields 1 A ◿
1 B ◺
4 D △

Diagram 5
Forming a hexagon from 60-degree triangles

FUSSY CUTTING

Sometimes you may wish to centre or make a feature of a motif. This is known as 'fussy cutting'. Use a commercial template with a cut-out centre, or make your own from template plastic, as shown in the photograph below. Be sure to include the seam allowance.

Mask off the seam allowance using masking tape to give yourself an accurate 'window' to look through. Place the template over the motif and move it around until you are happy with what you see. Trace lightly around the template with a pencil then cut out the shape.

To make the motif appear in the same place in each fussy-cut piece, mark the edges of the template to show where they overlap with particular elements in the design, then line up these marks with the relevant parts of the pattern on the fabric each time you cut a new piece.

Cutting shapes by hand

Shapes can be cut by hand using plastic or cardboard templates. This method is the most practical for curved shapes. When cutting fabric using templates, the template is generally made to its finished size, that is, without seam allowances; these are added when cutting the fabric. Commercially produced plastic templates are available in various shapes and sizes, or you can make your own templates from thin cardboard or template plastic (available from craft stores).

If using templates provided in a magazine or book, photocopy the template, paste it onto thin cardboard (card stock) and cut it out. Always check the template's dimensions for accuracy and adjust if need be before using it to cut fabric.

Place the template on the wrong side of the fabric and trace around it. (Placing the fabric face down onto a sheet of fine sandpaper first will prevent it from slipping about on the work surface when you trace around the template.) Use a sharp pencil or fine marker to give the finest line and thus the most accurate seam. This tracing line will become the seam line. Trace the required number of shapes, remembering to allow enough space between them for the seam allowance.

Cut out the shape, allowing a seam allowance of ¼ inch. Most of the time this can be calculated by eye, but tools are available to allow you to measure a precise ¼ inch seam allowance. On a straight-edged template, this can be done using a perspex quilter's quarter (see page 180). For a curved template, use a seam tracer. This is a small metal disc with a hole in the centre and a groove around the outside. You put a pencil in the hole and the edge of the disk against the edge of the template, and roll the seam tracer around the edge of the template to give a precise ¼ inch seam line. Another type of seam tracer consists of two connected pencils with their points ¼ inch apart; one is held against the edge of the template and the other is used to trace around it.

Below left: Using a piece of template plastic to act as a window when fussy-cutting a motif. **Below:** Tracing around a cardboard template on the back of the fabric, leaving space for a seam allowance between each shape, before cutting the shapes out.

APPLIQUÉ

There are various appliqué techniques; those used in this book are the iron-on method (right, used in Annie's Garden, page 62) and the needle-turn method (below, used in Holiday Morning, page 92, Summer Sunshine, page 98, and Fanciful Flowers, page 112). Whatever appliqué method you choose, complete all the appliqué before piecing the blocks together.

Before beginning the appliqué, decide where you want your shapes to sit on the background block. Use a sharp 2B pencil or other marker to lightly trace the shapes onto the background fabric. A light box is useful when tracing; if you don't have one, an alternative is to lightly tape the design to be traced onto a sunny window, lightly tape the fabric over it, then trace the design.

Remember that some designs will need to have their various elements sewn down in a particular order. For example, when sewing a flower, the stem will need to be sewn first so that it sits under the flower petals, then the petals added, and lastly the flower centre and the leaves. If you are working a complicated appliqué design and you think you might get confused, draw or photocopy a diagram of the complete design, determine the order in which the pieces need to be laid down, and then number the shapes on the diagram so you can keep track.

Needle-turn method

The first step is to trace the template shapes onto cardboard or template plastic using a very sharp 2B pencil. Using paper scissors, cut out along the line.

Place the template down on the front of the fabric and trace around it. Take care to leave space between the pieces for a seam allowance. Using sharp fabric scissors, cut the shapes out of the fabric a scant ¼ inch outside of the pencil line.

Using your fingers, press the edges of the fabric along the pencil line, making a sharp, smooth crease. Do not iron, as this will make points in the curves.

Fold the background square into halves, then quarters, and finger press the creases to find the centre of the block. Position the pieces on the background block using the diagram or photograph supplied with the pattern as a guide. Using short pins, pin the pieces to the background. Take into account which parts of the various pieces may go under others; dotted lines on the template pieces indicate which parts of each piece should be placed under the adjacent pieces.

Using thread to match the piece you are appliquéing, slip-stitch the piece to the background fabric. Your stitches should catch the edge of the fabric. Make your stitches as small as possible, and add an extra stitch to secure any points.

Turn the block over and make a small cut at the back of the shape, taking care not to cut the appliqué. Cut the background away underneath the flower. Be sure not to cut closer than ¼ inch away from the seam lines. Removing the fabric in this way makes the appliqué sit nicely and creates fewer layers to quilt through, especially where appliqué pieces overlap.

Repeat this process with each shape in turn. Remove the background from under each piece before applying the next one.

IRON-ON METHOD

This method requires Vliesofix, or double-sided fusible interfacing. Vliesofix has a paper side, which is smooth, and a webbing side, which is rough. Trace the desired shape onto the paper side of the Vliesofix and cut out roughly using paper scissors.

Using a hot iron, iron the roughly cut Vliesofix shapes onto the back of the fabrics, with the webbing side down. It is vital that the webbing side is down, or the shape will stick to your iron.

Using sharp fabric scissors, cut the shapes out of the fabric along the pencil line. Peel the paper off the fabric, leaving the webbing stuck to the back of the fabric. Turn the shapes right side up and position them onto your background fabric. Now iron the pieces down so that they stick to the background panel.

Hand or machine appliqué around the edges of the shapes. If you are appliquéing by machine, set your blanket stitch to a width of 1.5 and a length of 2. Try the stitch out on scrap fabric to ensure you are happy with the result, then stitch around the shapes as above.

HAND PIECING

Sometimes — such as when sewing small hexagons or other pieces with set-in seams — hand piecing is easier than machine piecing. When hand piecing, the fabric pieces are put together with the right sides facing and the seam lines (rather than the raw edges) even. Use a short, fine needle and a matching sewing thread. Begin sewing with a small backstitch, then sew along the seam line using a small running stitch. Every five or six stitches, take another backstitch for strength. End with another small backstitch, then fasten off.

PIECING

'Piecing' is the name given to sewing together all the separate components of a quilt. It can be done by hand or machine. To keep track of the various components, especially if making complicated blocks with many pieces, it is a good idea to put each type of piece in its own lock-seal plastic bag and label the bag. This also prevents the pieces from becoming lost, damaged, soiled or frayed.

Machine-piecing techniques

Piecing by machine requires accurate and precise seams (see page 178). The standard seam allowance is ¼ inch. If you plan to do a lot of machine piecing, a ¼ inch sewing-machine foot will be a good investment.

Machine-piecing is by its very nature much faster than hand-piecing, but by employing a technique called chain-piecing, you can make it faster still. To chain-piece, do not lift the presser foot and cut the thread each time you finish a seam. Instead, once you finish the seam on one unit (such as a pair of triangles, as shown below), sew a little beyond the end of the seam. The reel and bobbin threads will entwine to make a 'chain'. Put another unit under the presser foot and repeat the process until you have sewn all the units. Cut the chains between each unit and press the units open, pressing the seam toward the darker piece. Join the units to other components. Many parts of a quilt can be chain-pieced in this manner, saving both time and thread.

Far left, top: Beginning to chain-piece two half-square triangles. **Far left, bottom:** Once the seam on the first pair is complete, the next pair is fed into the machine without snipping the thread. **Left:** Continue in this manner to create strings of pairs. The 'chained' threads between the pairs are then cut and the units pressed open. **Opposite page, bottom:** Kathy pins blocks to a design wall to check for layout and colour balance.

QUILT LAYOUT AND ASSEMBLY

The quilt layout diagram provided in the pattern will show you how the various components are assembled. There are numerous ways of laying out a quilt. Diagrams 1 and 2 show two common layouts. In Diagram 1, blocks have been set square (that is, parallel with the sides and top of the quilt) and separated from one another by narrow rows of fabric known as sashing strips. Diagram 2 shows blocks set on point (at a 45-degree angle to the tops and sides of the quilt). This method requires the addition of triangles (known as setting triangles) at the corners and along the sides of the rows to square up the quilt.

Always refer to the layout diagram for the quilt you are making, rather than relying on a photograph. Many quilt designs, especially complex ones using more than one type of block, feature optical illusions caused by the way in which the various components are combined. Sometimes the logic of the quilt's construction will not become clear until you look at the layout diagram.

If you're making a scrappy quilt or one that has a lot of blocks of different colours or tones, it's a good idea to lay them all out on a flat surface such as the floor or a wall (or a design wall if you have one) and move the blocks about until you get a pleasing arrrangement. Check that the same fabrics aren't too close to each other, and that the eye is not drawn to particular blocks or areas at the expense of the rest of the design. Squinting at the quilt or looking at it through the lens of a camera can help you discern 'holes' or unbalanced areas.

Adding borders

Borders may be added for decorative effect, to increase the quilt's size, or both. They may have squared-off or mitred corners. The quilt pattern will tell you what length to cut the borders to, but you should always measure your quilt before cutting the border fabric, then adjust the length of the border strips if necessary.

Measure in both directions through the middle of the quilt rather than along the edges. This is because the edges may have distorted a little during the making of the quilt, especially if any of the edge pieces are bias cut. Use these measurements to calculate the length of each border, remembering to add a seam allowance.

If adding squared-off borders, the side borders will be the length of the quilt top, plus seam allowance. The top and bottom borders will be the width of the quilt top with the side borders added, plus seam allowance. Sew the side borders on first, press the seams towards the border, then add the top and bottom borders.

If adding borders with mitred corners, each border will need to be the width or length of the quilt, plus twice the width of the border to allow enough fabric for mitring, plus seam allowance. Sew each border to the edge of the quilt, beginning and ending the seam a precise ¼ inch (6 mm) from the edge of the quilt. Join the fabric at the corners at a 45-degree angle. Trim excess fabric and press the seam toward the border. If adding more than one mitred border, repeat for each border.

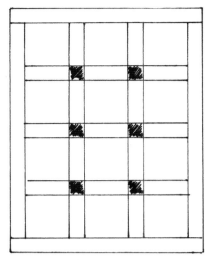

Diagram 1 **Square-set layout**

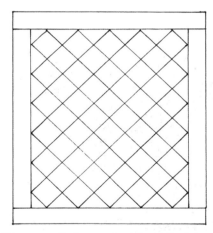

Diagram 2 **Layout set on point**

Layering the quilt

Once you have added all the borders, and before you can begin quilting, you will need to assemble all three layers of the quilt. This is known as layering or 'sandwiching' the quilt.

The wadding and backing should both be about 4 inches (10 cm) larger all round than the quilt top. (You may need to join two widths of lengths of fabric, or add a strip of scraps or leftover blocks, to obtain a large enough piece for the backing.)

Press the quilt top and backing. Lay the backing right side down on a large, flat, clean surface (preferably one that is not carpeted), smooth it out carefully, then tape it to the surface using masking tape. Tape it at intervals along all sides, but do not tape the corners, as this will cause the bias to stretch out of shape.

Place the wadding on top of the backing and smooth it out. If you need to join two pieces of wadding, butt them up together and then machine zigzag a seam.

On top of the wadding, place the well-pressed quilt top, right side up, ensuring that the top and backing are square to each other. Smooth it out.

The three layers must now be basted ready for quilting (see opposite).

Below left: The pressed backing fabric is laid face down on the floor, smoothed out and taped down. **Below centre:** The wadding is placed on top of the backing. **Below:** The pressed quilt top is placed face up on top of the wadding.

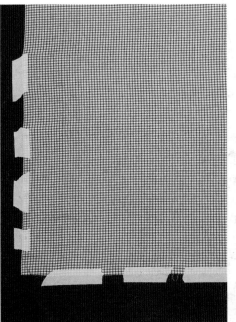

Basting

Basting holds the layers in place while the quilt is quilted. Basting can be done with safety pins or long hand stitches.

If using safety pins, start from the centre of the quilt and pin through all three layers at intervals of about 8 inches (20 cm). If you are intending to machine-quilt, make sure the pins are kept away from the lines to be quilted. Once the whole quilt is safety-pinned in this manner, it can be moved. Safety pins can be used for hand-quilting, but be mindful that they can get in the way of your hoop.

If you are intending to hand-quilt, baste (tack) the whole quilt both horizontally and vertically, from the centre out, using long hand stitches at intervals of about 6 inches (15 cm). Using a curved needle is a good idea, as this makes the task easier on the wrists. If you're basting a quilt on a carpeted surface, using a curved needle also helps avoid running the basting stitches into the carpet.

Do not baste using hand stitches if you intend to machine quilt, as the basting threads will get caught under the presser foot.

Some quilting stores offer a machine basting service. This can be a worthwhile investment, especially if you are going to be doing fine hand quilting in the traditional manner, a task that can take months or even years.

Remove the basting stitches or safety pins only once all the quilting is complete.

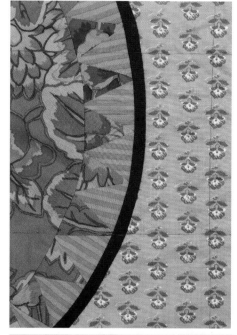

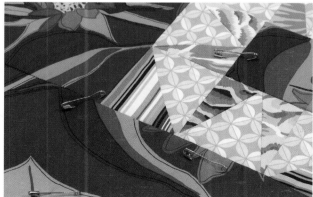

Top right: A quilt that has been commercially machine basted using long stitches. **Above:** Basting using safety pins. **Right:** Hand basting using a curved needle.

Ditch-stitching (or stitching in the ditch) is the term given to quilting along a seamline. This gives a subtle effect, as the sewing is hidden in the seam.

Machine ditch-stitching is quick to do, but it can be difficult to maintain an absolutely straight line. The best strategy is to sew slowly and patiently to avoid running off the track.

Because a seam is pressed in one direction, it has a high side and a low side. Quilting should be done on the low side of a seam, so that the stitching only needs to penetrate three layers instead of five.

Below: Avalon (see page 16) was quilted in a continuous floral design using a commercial long-arm machine. Such machines are moved around over the quilt, rather than the quilt having to be moved under the machine as is the case with domestic sewing machines.

QUILTING

Quilting can be fairly rudimentary, its main purpose being to hold together the layers of the quilt, or it can be decorative and sometimes extremely elaborate. Machine-quilting is quick, but nothing beats hand-quilting for sheer heirloom beauty.

Designs for hand-quilting, or elaborate designs for machine-quilting, are generally marked on the quilt top before the quilt's layers are sandwiched together. On pale fabrics, the marking is done lightly in pencil; on dark fabrics, use a special quilter's silver pencil. Pencil lines can be erased later.

If you intend to quilt straight lines or a cross-hatched design, masking tape can be used to mark out the lines on the quilt top. Such tape comes in various widths, from ¼ inch upwards. Free-flowing lines can be drawn on with a chalk pencil.

If you intend to outline-quilt by machine, you may be able to sew straight enough lines by eye; if not, you will need to mark the quilt top first. There is no need to mark the quilt top if you intend only to machine-quilt in the ditch (see left).

Machine-quilting

You will need a walking foot for your machine; these ensure that the fabric on both the top and the bottom of the quilt feeds through evenly. Walking feet can be bought from sewing machine and some craft suppliers. To avoid puckers and distortion of the quilt, machine-quilting should commence in the centre of the quilt and proceed outwards to the edges.

Find the spot to begin quilting. Bring the bobbin thread up to the surface of the quilt and machine-sew ¼ inch of very small stitches to secure the thread and prevent the quilting from unravelling, then quilt with stitches at the normal length. When you reach ¼ inch from the end of the quilting line, again sew with very small stitches. Clip all the threads to the surface.

Straight or walking-foot quilting should be tackled first. Quilt from the centre point to the border edge. Turn the quilt 90 degrees and stitch again from the centre to the border edge. Repeat for the remaining sides until you have quilted all the straight lines. Then go back and ditch-quilt or outline-quilt the blocks.

For free-motion quilting, change to a darning foot and drop the feed dogs. Follow the marked lines of your design, or stipple-quilt by moving the fabric around so that the quilting forms a random, meandering pattern.

To make the bulk of the quilt easier to manoeuvre, roll up one side of the quilt so that it fits neatly under the machine. Unroll and reroll as necessary as you proceed from one part of the design to another.

Hand-quilting

Quilting by hand produces a softer line than machine-quilting, and will give an heirloom quality to quilts. Most of the quilts in this book are quilted using perle cotton, although traditional quilting thread can be used if you prefer.

To quilt by hand, the fabric needs to be held in a frame (also known as a quilting hoop). Free-standing frames are available, but hand-held ones are cheaper, more portable and just as effective. One edge of a hand-held frame can be leaned against a table or bench to enable you to keep both hands free.

Hand quilting, like machine quilting, should commence in the centre of the quilt and proceed outward. To commence hand quilting, place the plain (inner) ring of the frame under the centre of the quilt. Position the other ring, with the screw, over the top of the quilt to align with the inner ring. Tighten the screw so that the fabric in the frame becomes firm, but not drum-tight.

For traditional quilting, choose the smallest needle that you feel comfortable with. For perle quilting, use a good-quality crewel embroidery needle. Thread the needle with about 18 inches (45 cm) of thread. Knot the end of the thread and take the needle down through the quilt top into the wadding, a short distance from where you want to start quilting. Tug the thread slightly so that the knot pulls through into the wadding, making the starting point invisible. Proceed as follows.

THE HAND-QUILTING ACTION

With your dominant hand above the quilt and the other beneath, insert the needle through all three layers at a time with the middle or index finger of your dominant hand (use a metal thimble to make this easier) until you can feel the tip of the needle resting on your finger at the back. Without pushing the needle through, rock the needle back to the top of the quilt and use your underneath finger to push the tip of the needle up. Put your upper thumb down in front of the needle tip while pushing up from the back. This will make a small 'hill' in the fabric. Push the needle through the fabric. This makes one stitch. To take several stitches at once, push the needle along to the required stitch length then dip the tip into the fabric and repeat the above technique. Gently pull the stitches to indent the stitch line evenly. You should always quilt toward yourself, as this reduces hand and shoulder strain, so turn the quilt in the required direction. You can protect your underneath finger using a stick-on plastic shield such as a Thimble-It. You can also use a leather thimble; however, this does make it more difficult to feel how far the needle has come through, and thus more difficult to keep your stitches even.

To move a short distance from one part of the quilting design to another, push the tip of the needle through the wadding and up at the new starting point. Take care not to drag a dark thread under a light fabric, as the line will show.

When you come to the edge of the hoop, leave the thread dangling so that you can pick it up and continue working with it once you have repositioned the hoop. Work all the quilting design within the hoop before repositioning the hoop and beginning to quilt another area. If you need to quilt right up to the border edge, baste lengths of spare cotton fabric to the edge of the quilt, thus giving you enough fabric area to position the edges of the quilt under the quilting hoop.

To fasten off a length of thread, see right.

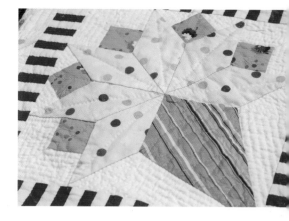

Above: Surprise Package (see page 162) was hand-quilted in the traditional manner using fine waxed quilting thread and small stitches. **Below:** Detail of hand-quilting on Strawberry Fields (see page 146) using perle cotton.

FINISHING A THREAD

Hold the thread out to the side with your left hand, and loop a one-loop knot using the needle. Slide the loose knot down the thread until it lies directly on the quilt top, and tighten the knot. Take the needle back down through the hole the thread is coming out of and slide it away through the wadding. Bring the needle back up to the top of the quilt and give the thread a tug. The knot will follow down into the hole and lodge in the wadding. Cut the thread close to the surface.

BINDING

From the width of the binding fabric, cut enough strips of fabric to equal the outside edge of your quilt, plus about 6 in (15 cm) to allow for mitred corners and for the ends to be folded under. Binding fabrics are usually (though not always) cut into strips 2½ inches wide; follow the instructions in the pattern.

Seam the strips into a continuous length, making the joins at 45-degree angles as shown below. To do this, fold under one end at a 45-degree angle and finger-press a crease. Unfold. The crease line will become the seam line. Mark this line lightly with a pencil. With right sides together and the two fabric pieces at 90 degrees, align the angled cut end with another strip of binding fabric. Align the ¼ inch measurement on a quilter's ruler with this line and trim off the corner. Sew the two strips together along the marked line. Press all seams to one side and trim off the 'ears'.

Press the entire strip in half along its length. Doubling the fabric like this makes the binding more durable.

Trim the backing and the wadding so that they are even with the edge of the quilt top. Beginning at one end of the binding strip, pin the binding to one edge of the quilt, starting about 4 inches (10 cm) in from a corner and having raw edges even. Machine-sew in place through all the layers of the quilt, using a ¼ inch seam allowance and mitring the corners. To mitre corners, end the seam ¼ inch from the corner and fasten off. Fold the binding fabric up at a 45-degree angle, then fold it down so that the fold is level with the edge of the binding just sewn. Begin the next seam at the edge of the quilt and proceed as before. Repeat this process to mitre all the corners.

When you approach the point at which the binding started, trim the excess, tuck the end of the binding under itself (as shown opposite, bottom centre) and stitch the rest of the seam.

Press the binding away from the quilt. Turn the binding to the back of the quilt and blind hem stitch in place by hand to finish. Your quilt is now complete!

Below: Preparing to join two lengths of binding fabric at a 45-degree angle. **Below right:** The finished join, ready to be pressed to one side.

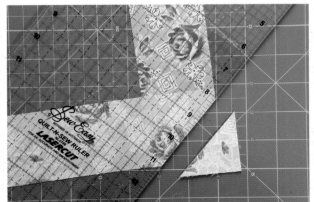

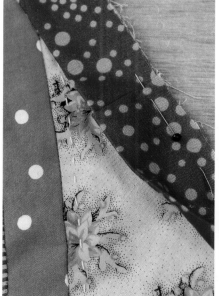

Above: Detail of the backing and binding of Dotty for Dresden (see page 120). **Below:** Machine sewing the binding to the front of the quilt. **Right:** When you approach the point at which the binding begins, fold the end under to make a neat finish. **Far right:** Slip-stitching the binding to the back of the quilt.

glossary,

index

Glossary

APPLIQUÉ A technique in which small pieces of fabric are attached to a background fabric. They may be stitched on by hand or by machine, or ironed on using fusible webbing.

BACKING The undermost layer of a quilt, often a plain piece of fabric.

BASTING A method of holding together several layers of fabric during quilting, so that they do not move around. Basting may be done using a long hand stitch, or with safety pins. The stitches or pins are removed once the quilting is complete.

BATTING Another term for wadding; the middle layer of a quilt.

BIAS The diagonal of a woven fabric, at a 45-degree angle to the straight grains (the warp and weft). Fabric cut on the bias stretches, so care must be taken when handling and sewing bias-cut pieces.

BINDING The narrow strips of fabric (usually made of a double thickness) that enclose the raw edges and batting of a quilt.

BLOCK The basic unit of a quilt top. Blocks are usually square, but may be rectangular, hexagonal or other shapes. They may be plain (of one fabric only), appliquéd or pieced.

BORDER A strip of fabric (plain, appliquéd or pieced) joined to the central panel of a quilt and used to frame it and also to add extra size.

CHAIN PIECING A method of joining fabric pieces by machine in an assembly-line fashion, which speeds up the process and uses less thread. Pairs or sets of block pieces are fed into the machine one after the other, without snipping the threads between them.

CROSS HATCHING A quilting pattern of parallel equidistant lines that run in two directions to form a grid of squares or diamonds.

DIRECTIONAL PRINT Printed fabric in which there is a distinct direction to the pattern, whether straight or at an angle; for example, stripes, human or animal figures, or some florals.

EASE To make two pieces of fabric of different size fit together in the one seam. One piece may have to be stretched or gathered slightly to bring it to the required length. To ease, first pin the pieces at intervals until they fit, then sew them.

FAT QUARTER A piece of fabric that is made by cutting a metre or a yard of fabric in halves first vertically then horizontally. The piece thus cut is approximately 50 x 56 cm or 18 x 22 inches.

FEED DOGS The teeth under the sewing plate of a sewing machine, which move to pull the fabric through the machine. The feed dogs must be raised to allow for free-motion quilting.

FINGER-PRESSING A way of pressing a temporary crease in a piece of fabric, for example when finding the middle of two pieces so that they can be matched before being joined. Running a fingernail along a crease will make it lie flat.

FOUR-PATCH A block with two, four or multiples of four units per block.

FUSIBLE WEBBING A fabric that has been coated with an adhesive that fuses fabric pieces together when pressed with a warm iron. Such products may be fusible on only one side (Vilene or fusible interfacing), or both (Vliesofix). Fusible webbing is used to stabilise fine fabrics or to attach appliqué pieces to the background fabric.

FUSSY CUTTING A method of selectively cutting a piece of fabric so as to showcase a particular motif, such as a large flower. Fussy cutting is most easily done using a see-through template that allows you to position the motif to best advantage within the template area.

GRAIN The direction of the fabric, along the warp (vertical threads) or the weft (horizontal threads). These are both straight grains, along which woven fabrics do not stretch. Compare with Bias.

HALF-SQUARE TRIANGLE A triangle that is made from a square cut across one diagonal. Half-square triangles have the bias along the hypotenuse. Compare with Quarter-square triangle.

LOFT A term referring to the thickness of wadding (batting). A high-loft wadding is thicker and fluffier than a low-loft wadding.

MITRED CORNER A corner that is joined at a 45-degree angle.

MOTIF A design element or image used in a printed fabric, quilt block or appliqué block, for example a heart motif or floral motif.

MUSLIN A plain, usually undyed cotton fabric that may be bleached or unbleached. A fine-weave muslin, known as quilter's muslin, is often used as the background for appliqué or quilt blocks.

NOVELTY PRINT A fabric printed with themed designs, such as toys, cartoon characters or animals.

ONE-PATCH Any quilt design that uses a single shaped piece, such as a hexagon, square or triangle, for the pieced top.

ON POINT An arrangement in which the quilt blocks are placed diamond fashion, with their corners at the 12, 3, 6 and 9 o'clock positions, rather than in a square fashion.

OUTLINE QUILT To make one or more outlines of a motif or block design, radiating outwards.

PATCH See Piece.

PATCHWORK A generic term for the process of sewing together many small pieces of fabric to make a quilt. Also known as piecework.

PIECE An individual fabric shape that may be joined to other fabric shapes to make a quilt block, or used on its own (in which case it is known as a one-patch). Also known as a patch.

PIECING The process of joining together pieces of fabric to make a quilt top, a quilt block, or a border.

PIN-BASTE To pin through the layers of a quilt 'sandwich', using safety pins, to hold them together during quilting. The pins are removed once the quilting is complete.

QUARTER-SQUARE TRIANGLE A triangle that is made from a square cut across both diagonals. Quarter-square triangles have the bias along the two short sides.

QUILT TOP The uppermost, decorative layer of a quilt. It may be pieced, appliquéd or a combination of both, with or without borders.

QUILTER'S RULERS Precision-cut, straight-edged plastic rulers in various sizes, used with rotary cutters and rotary cutting mats. They make it easy to cut accurate shapes, and to cut through several layers of fabric at once. They come in straight varieties and also those designed for cutting at various angles or for creating triangles.

QUILTING In general, the process of making a quilt; more specifically, the process of stitching patterns by hand or machine into the quilt layers to decorate the quilt, add strength and anchor the wadding inside the quilt.

QUILTING FRAME A free-standing floor apparatus, made of wood or plastic tubing, in which a quilt is held while it is being quilted.

QUILTING HOOP A hand-held circular wooden device in which a quilt is held while being quilted.

RAW EDGE The cut edge of a fabric.

ROTARY CUTTER A cutting device similar in appearance to a pizza cutter, with a razor-sharp circular blade. Used in conjunction with a quilter's ruler, it allows several layers of fabric to be cut at once, easily and with great accuracy.

ROTARY CUTTING MAT Self-healing plastic mat on which rotary cutters are used, to protect both the blade of the cutter and the work surface beneath the mat.

SASHING Strips of fabric that separate blocks in a quilt, to frame them and/or make the quilt larger.

SEAM ALLOWANCE The margin of fabric between the cut edge and the seam line. For quilting and most appliqué, it is ¼ inch.

SEAM LINE The guideline that is followed while sewing.

SELVEDGES The finished edges along the length of the fabric.

SETTING The way in which blocks are arranged in a quilt top, for example square or on point.

SETTING SQUARE Plain block or square used with pieced or appliquéd blocks in a quilt top.

SETTING TRIANGLE A triangle placed between blocks along the side of a quilt set on point, to straighten up the edges.

STASH A quilter's hoard of fabrics.

TEMPLATE Plastic, cardboard or paper shape used for tracing and cutting fabric pieces for piecing or applique, or to transfer quilting designs to a quilt top.

WALKING FOOT A special sewing-machine foot that feeds the top layer of a quilt sandwich evenly through the machine, while the feed dogs control the bottom layer.

WARP The lengthwise threads in a woven fabric, which interlock with the weft threads. See also Weft.

WEFT The widthwise threads in a woven fabric, which interlock with the warp threads. See also Warp.

Index

STOCKISTS

Fabrics, kits and accessories
are available from Material
Obsession, 144 Pittwater Road,
Gladesville NSW 2110 Australia
Phone (+61 2) 9817 2733
www.materialobsession.com

Prints Charming panels are
available from Prints Charming
(www.printscharming.com.au) or
from Material Obsession, above.

About the authors

Kathy Doughty

Quilting has always been about the promise of joy for me. Although I grew up in Ohio, where quilting is a way of life for many, I never really took much notice of quilts. They were a part of the background of my life and the history of my country. Unlike many of my quilting peers, I was a sewing-badge flunky, a home economics failure and the one most likely to be hanging upside down from a tree branch as a kid.

I migrated to Australia after marrying an Australian. One of my first friends gave us a quilt that she and her daughter had made when our second son, Noah, was born. Time stopped as I held the quilt in my hands and marvelled at the feeling the carefully chosen bits of fabric gave me. From that moment on, I was a quilter.

After several years, I joined Hunters Hill Quilt group in Sydney, where I met Sarah Fielke, who would soon become my business partner in a patchwork shop. The quilt group offered companionship with like-minded, similarly obsessed women, and so much more. A quilt group brings us back to a time where women talked and shared stories of their lives. This group of individuals has given me a home away from home that adds real quality to my life.

My quilts are often a journey of revelation that starts out headed in a specific direction but ends up somewhere completely different. Fabric, colour and graphics take me on their path, rather than the other way around. As a teacher of patchwork, I like to encourage people to listen to their inner self and make choices that suit them, that they like, that are personal. After all, a quilt is simply the personal expression of one's inner self; each step makes it your own, and each mistake personalises it.

I choose to work with colours off the primary scale. I like them to engage the eye because they aren't a perfect match, but rather a combination that takes the eye on a journey of discovery. Some people find my quilts 'busy', which is a concept I love. Quilts have always been a reflection of a woman's life and our society, and mine are a reflection of the chaotic times in which we live. Things move quickly and clutter is the new neutral. Every day an image engages the eye and the brain starts to work out how to transform that image into a quilt.

Quilting has always involved sampling a bit of something, mixing it up with a bit of something else and making it your own thing. The choices are infinite, the options limitless, the results various and delightful. Quilting is a diverse and endless area of learning that can occupy our hands and minds throughout our lives.

Sarah Fielke

I was raised in Sydney, Australia, about as far from a traditional centre of quilting as you can get. Despite this, as I grew up, Australian quilting was flourishing and coming into its own, and beginning to be the creative and internationally recognised community it is now.

My mother had sewn her whole life and came to quilting in her thirties. The first quilt she made was for me, when I was four years old, and I promptly cut it up. After all, Mum was always cutting things up with her big, heavy, silver sewing shears, and from the first I wanted in.

My mother died a few years ago, and quilting has become an enjoyable and necessary part of my life. It is also a way of connecting to my mother, and to the thousands of quilters who make quilting so personal, and yet so much part of a greater whole. Through my mother, the business, my students, and my quilt group, I have a sense of belonging that I have never felt elsewhere.

My quilts are about today's world, but rather than reflecting the busyness of life, they often provide a quiet place to rest. They make use of space and light as well as pattern. I like to combine modern, clear colours and contemporary fabrics with traditional blocks to weave together history and present times.

Quilting is a sanctuary into which I retreat from the daily bustle. I can lose myself in the rhythm of stitches and repetition of piecing, and take myself out of the moment using colours, textures and patterns. Quilting is my peace and quiet, my personal space.

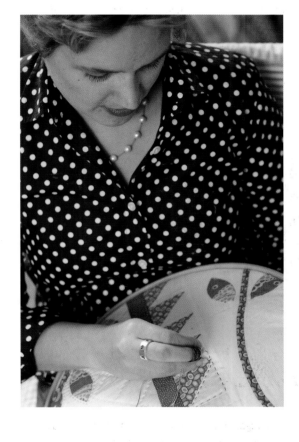

Acknowledgments

Kathy would like to thank:

John Doughty, for sharing his critical eye, for the photos that capture the feeling of what we do and for his untiring support in life. • Oscar, Noah and Sam, for being beautiful boys ... talking to me while I work on my projects and never complaining that all I do is quilt. • Sarah, for sharing her talent and her friendship and for the obvious reason that we work so well together to make Material Obsession what it is today. • Who doesn't thank their mom and dad ... mom, for teaching me to be a woman with an eye for colour, and dad, for teaching me how to be real. • Bronwyn Goesling, who taught me how to quilt in the first place. • Kaffe Fassett, for giving me an ideal to aspire to in use of colour and design.

Sarah would like to thank:

Damian Fielke, for his unfailing love, support and enthusiasm for everything I do, and for his energy and ideas for both the business and our family. • Charlie and Oscar, for being the lights in my life and my greatest quilting critics. • Kathy, for hunting me down and beginning the MO partnership for both of us. We've had such fun together — and much more! • My mother, who taught me to sew, to love and to believe that I can be anything I want to be. Also to her mother, who made all three of us strong women.

We would both like to thank:

Justin and Wendy Doughty, for the use of their farm in Mudgee for the photography. • Geoffrey and Darleen Cousins, for the use of the beach house. • Kim Bradley and her trusty partner Dave, for providing us with an excellent and creative quilting service. • Erica Spinks and Clare Mooney, for supporting us in their magazines and for being such great women to work with. • Sally Harding, Sheena Chapman, Bundle (Louise) Caldwell and Florence Tynan, our wonderful shop girls. • Special thanks go to Carolyn Davis, for helping us in the shop since the day we opened, making it possible for us to do what we do, her unfailing belief in our success and her wonderful friendship. • Lastly, all the girls at Hunters Hill Quilt group, for creating a community in which to quilt and share life stories, because ultimately, that's what it's all about.

206 ❈ Material Obsession

Published in 2008 by Murdoch Books Pty Limited

Murdoch Books Australia
Pier 8/9
23 Hickson Road
Millers Point NSW 2000
Phone: +61 (0) 2 8220 2000
Fax: +61 (0) 2 8220 2558
www.murdochbooks.com.au

Murdoch Books UK Limited
Erico House, 6th Floor
93–99 Upper Richmond Road
Putney, London SW15 2TG
Phone: +44 (0) 20 8785 5995
Fax: +44 (0) 20 8785 5985
www.murdochbooks.co.uk

Chief Executive: Juliet Rogers
Publishing Director: Kay Scarlett

Design Manager: Vivien Valk
Commissioning editor: Kay Scarlett
Project manager and editor: Janine Flew
Design concept and designer: Tracy Loughlin
Production: Kita George

National Library of Australia Cataloguing-in-Publication Data
Doughty, Kathy.
Material Obsession / authors, Kathy Doughty and Sarah Fielke.
Sydney, N.S.W. : Murdoch Books, 2008.
9781741960952 (pbk.)
Includes index.
Quilting —Patterns. Patchwork quilts. Patchwork — Patterns.
Fielke, Sarah.
746.46

Colour separation by Splitting Image
Printed by i-Book Printing Ltd in 2008. PRINTED IN CHINA.